Green
Business

■

WITHDRAWN

Green Business

Making it Work for Your Company

■

MALCOLM WHEATLEY

the Institute
of Management

PITMAN PUBLISHING

Pitman Publishing
128 Long Acre, London WC2E 9AN

A Division of Longman Group UK Limited

The
publisher's
policy is to use
paper manufactured
from sustainable forests

First published in 1993

© Malcolm Wheatley 1993

A CIP catalogue record for this book can be obtained
from the British Library

ISBN 0 273 60020 6

Photoset in Linotron Century Schoolbook by
Northern Phototypesetting Co., Ltd., Bolton
Printed by Bell and Bain Ltd, Glasgow

Contents

■

Foreword

■

This book is a practical guide on environmental management for today's managers. Few of them will have failed to have noticed the media coverage of environmental problems, and many will have studied the international agreements, such as those reached at the Earth Summit in 1992 and the growing body of legislation extending the statutory responsibilities of companies.

However compliance with the law, and indeed achievement of targets and timescales for identified initiatives, requires proper management. Profit becomes pointless without quality of life, but a greener future will remain an idealistic dream unless industry becomes increasingly aware of its basic responsibilities.

The Laing Group has long had a philosophy of putting something back into the community. As part of this we have adopted sound business sense when tackling environmental problems.

Whether it's a question of good housekeeping, urging green practices on clients and suppliers, or supplying objective information to the general public, companies in the 21st century will as a matter of course include environmental management in their business plans.

As always, new challenges will mean change, but with added opportunities leading to survival, success and ultimately a better environment.

JMK Laing CBE
Chairman, John Laing plc
and Chairman, WWF UK (World Wide Fund For Nature)

Acknowledgements

■

A book of this nature inevitably draws heavily on the work of those who have gone before. Not all their contributions can be acknowledged, but it does seem especially appropriate to thank John Gribbin, Mark Carwardine, Colin Tudge and Walter Patterson, who have done so much to stimulate people's awareness over the years. Particular thanks are due to various people at Friends of the Earth and WWF, especially Gill Witter. The work of Tom Handler of Baker & McKenzie, who kindly advised on various legal matters, is also gratefully acknowledged.

ix

*The opinions expressed in this book
do not necessarily represent those
of WWF or its associates.*

WWF aims to conserve nature and ecological processes by:

- preserving genetic, species, and ecosystem diversity;
- ensuring that the use of renewable natural resources is sustainable both now and in the longer term;
- promoting actions to reduce pollution and the wasteful exploitation and consumption of resources.

WWF – World Wide Fund For Nature – is the world's largest private international conservation organisation with 28 Affiliate and Associate National Organisations around the world and over 5.2 million regular supporters. WWF continues to be known as World Wildlife Fund in Canada and the United States of America.

Why the environment matters

Before looking at the role business plays in the environment, we first examine what is happening to the earth – and why people are worried about it.

- **what is 'going green' all about – and why does it matter?**

- **the key ecological problems: preserving the biosphere and its genetic diversity, and husbanding the earth's resources**

- **putting the pieces into place: the 'greenhouse effect', acid rain, energy efficiency, recycling, pollution and wildlife**

- **how bad is the situation – and in which direction are things moving?**

Hacking through the greenery

This is not a book written by an idealist or dreamer. A product of the mid-Fifties 'baby boom', I am old enough to remember how things used to be – and how they've changed since, sometimes for the better, sometimes not. We can fantasise about the technologies of my grandfather's day – who, in his early years as a farmer, still used shire horses – but never really go back to them. Technology has irrevocably changed so many aspects of working life – these words, for example, are being typed into a laptop computer on board a train as I travel to a business meeting. The frenetic pace of technology's progress has brought us new conveniences and broadened our horizons at breakneck speed. Next week, business takes me to the US for a few days: a generation ago, just the journey there – by sea, of course – would have been as long as my entire trip will take. Transatlantic travel has become as commonplace as European travel.

Yet the legacy of both journeys is undoubted environmental damage – the very act of travel brings about the consumption of irreplacable fossil fuels, atmospheric pollution, damage to the ozone layer and the production of greenhouse gases. The trail of litter and rubbish will be just as bad – plastic coffee cups, burger wrappers, 'one shot' cream containers and all the other paraphernalia of modern day mastication on the move.

But this is *not* a book that advocates radically espoused alternatives. It is not going to advocate managers donning smocks and cycling to meetings instead. It *is* a book that points out *practical* green alternatives where such exist. Throughout, I have tried to restrict green ideas to the practically possible. Fifteen years' experience managing people in manufacturing industry and management consultancy has taught me how difficult it can be to make even the simplest changes.

But change there will have to be. Going green, for mankind as a whole, is no longer an option. As this first chapter tries to show, things are already badly awry with the earth's systems. A civilisation built on two fundamental assumptions – that resources last forever, and that the earth has a limitless capacity to heal itself – is in for an awful shock.

Yet 'going green' means different things to different people. For some people, it's a question of saving whales and rain forests. Other people get worked up more about energy or transport issues – fuel efficiency, nuclear power and leaded petrol. Still others find themselves arguing passionately in favour of recycling and pollution control. Nor does the list end with these. There are plenty more green issues around – pesticides in the food chain, fisheries conservation, and the depletion of the ozone layer.

People's reasons for going green are just as diverse. Some people regard it as an ethical issue. They want to preserve the Earth for future generations and get upset at the needless pain and suffering endured by whales and dolphins. Others see it as a health issue: air pollution, leaking toxic waste dumps, ozone depletion and food chain contamination. Waste upsets some people – for them the green movement's 'closed system', with every bit of rubbish and industrial byproduct being re-incarnated as something once again of use, has a certain harmony.

One of the lessons we have to learn about going green is that this sort of pigeonholing is wrong. Recycling nuts have to care just as deeply about rainforests, radiation and rhinoceroses. This was one of the key points made by the World Conservation Strategy, developed back in 1980 by a partnership of the UN, WWF and the World Conservation Union. The Strategy set down some of the guiding principles of the green movement that had emerged in the 1960s and 1970s in a single coherent form, and laid the foundations for what was to build up in the 1980s to today's broadly shared concern about environmental issues. Carrying as it did the endorsement of three respected bodies – including the United Nations – it did a lot to make environmentalism respectable. Green activists were no longer peculiar people wearing sandals and waving banners; they were ordinary people making decisions about the products that they bought and the sort of society in which they wanted to live.

3

The Strategy emphasised three objectives:

- it was essential that the world's fundamental ecological processes and life support systems be maintained

- the earth's genetic diversity must be preserved

- the use of the planet's resources and ecosystems must be *sustainable.*

Let's look at each of these in more detail.

PRESERVING ECOLOGICAL PROCESSES AND LIFE-SUPPORT SYSTEMS

This certainly sounds laudable enough. But how much real danger are they in to begin with? And what are the consequences of *not* preserving them? The answer to both questions, unfortunately, is that nobody really knows. But that shouldn't be cause for complacency.

Let's try and put it in context with a simple analogy. The world, let's say, is a bus, happily winding its way down a mountain road. Some of the passengers are unhappy about the speed at which the bus is travelling, and are pointing out the possible dangers. Nobody has been hurt yet – but they could be. The bus might crash into a roadside boulder – damaging it and injuring or killing some of the passengers – or it might plunge off the road completely, to certain destruction and the death of all on board. To make matters worse, although *some* of the passengers are complaining, others are not. They are happy with the speed, because they want to get to their destination faster. The driver doesn't know who to listen to – but is becoming conscious of the fact that if the worriers are right, by the time he does slow down it might be too late. There's no point slamming on the brakes when the bus has already gone over the precipice.

It's a pretty reasonable analogy. Take the well known green-house effect for example. At the time of writing, it cannot be shown that it has killed a single soul – despite the enormous brouhaha made about it. It may well take another ten or twenty years before it can even be proved – with the ninety-nine per cent statistical certainty that scientists require with these things – to be taking place at all. All we have at the moment are signs. The 1980s were the hottest decade on record, with drought wiping out the US grain harvest in 1988. 1992 sees much of Britain in its fourth consecutive year of below average rainfall, with summer drought conditions in the South and East as a result. Global sea levels are rising and so on.

All of these signs are certainly consistent with the climatic models that scientists have developed – but there isn't as yet any real conclusive *proof*. What we do know, though, is that the factors which in theory lead to the greenhouse effect are in place and continue to strengthen. Carbon dioxide, a heat-retentive gas, continues to be pumped into the atmosphere through human activities – chiefly the burning of fossil fuels – at the rate of around twenty-three billion tonnes a year. The world's forests – especially the tropical ones – act (quite literally) as 'lungs', converting this back into oxygen and vegetation. They are however, quickly vanishing. A third of the earth's girdle of tropical rainforest had gone by the Seventies; a further 170,000 square kilometres – that's an area about the size of England, Wales and Northern Ireland – is cut back every year. The weight of scientific evidence led over 150 countries to sign the Climatic Change Convention requiring reductions in their emissions of carbon dioxide, at the Earth Summit in 1992. The EC and the UK have already set themselves a target of bringing their carbon dioxide emission levels back to 1990 levels by the year 2000, with further reductions after that.

What's more, carbon dioxide is only one of a number of green-

5

house gases. Methane, historically known as 'swamp gas', is another one. It is a byproduct of many human agricultural activities in one form or another. Cows, for example, both burp and fart large quantities; rice paddies – in effect artificial swamps – contribute more. But it is man-made chloro-fluorocarbon gases that are a bigger menace. These, the so-called 'CFC' gases, were invented in the late 1920s and rapidly found a wide variety of industrial uses such as refrigerator coolants, aerosol propellants and polystyrene packaging. Adding a single molecule of a CFC gas to the atmosphere contributes ten thousand times more to the greenhouse effect than adding a single molecule of carbon dioxide and over 1.2 million tonnes of CFCs are produced every year. Not all of them escape directly into the atmosphere, of course. Clearly, those used as aerosol propellants do so virtually immediately. Those that are used in refrigerators take longer. The problem isn't that they leak from the cooling tubes at the back of refrigerator while it's in use, but that they do so once the fridge has been scrapped. Junked in a landfill, left to rust on wasteland, or recycled through a scrap merchant, the CFCs do ultimately get into the atmosphere. Ironically, it can be more beneficial to the environment to reclaim the previously disregarded CFCs than the copper and steel that have previously been recycled from abandoned and obsolete refrigerators.

And what we call the 'greenhouse effect' is only *one* of the earth's life-support systems going awry. CFCs, it turns out, are also responsible for destroying the earth's ozone layer, the atmospheric 'shield' that filters out a lot of the sun's harmful ultra-violet (UV) radiation. A case of slapping on a bit more sun cream and slipping on a pair of sun glasses? Not quite. Ever tried rubbing Factor 8 onto a cow – or telling it to keep its sunglasses on, otherwise it might go blind? Not that it will have much to graze on, anyway – too much UV stunts crop growth, reduces leaf size and impairs seed quality, as well as increasing plants' susceptibility to disease. Research also indicates that excessive UV can kill off a lot of the sea's tiny planktonic creatures. These are at the very bottom of the aquatic food chain that ultimately ends up on our dinner plates. The consequences of the present day rate of destruction of the ozone layer can be very serious indeed – but no one really knows *how* serious. In terms of the bus analogy again, it is certainly giving cause for concern. The degree of concern exhibited can best be judged by the fact that fifty countries have so far signed something called the Montreal Protocol for the Control of Ozone Depleting Substances. At their latest meeting, in Copenhagen in 1992, these countries agreed to a complete phase-out of CFC production by 1996, in the light of strong scientific evidence – including ozone depletion over the Northern hemisphere – that the problem is growing even more serious.

Clearly, tampering with the earth's inbuilt life-support mechanisms – and we have still only looked at the threats to two of them – is potentially very dangerous indeed. Any sensible person (committed environmentalist or not) should view with extreme disquiet any significant interference with their workings – hence the disavowal of such in the World Conservation Strategy. Let's now turn to the second guiding principle espoused by Greens.

PRESERVING THE EARTH'S GENETIC DIVERSITY

Until the 1992 Earth Summit in Rio de Janeiro, the concept of biodiversity had made little headway in the general public's appreciation of green issues. Saving ourselves, fine. Saving other species – well, does it *really* matter? Again, the answer is less than unequivocal. Science has catalogued and named around 1.4 million species of plant and animal. It's difficult to say, but there may be around thirty million species on the planet in total. Yet, at the rate of around 100 per day – although published estimates differ widely – species are being wiped out, gone forever.

But with so many around, why should we be worried? It is admittedly a complex and difficult question to answer. For a start, our global heritage – the world that we pass onto our children – is certainly theoretically poorer by their loss. These are not necessarily obscure plants and insects that we are talking about – the list of highly threatened species includes well known ones such as the giant panda, the mountain gorilla, the Californian condor and the humpbacked whale. The list of species that are less highly threatened, but still in danger, is much longer. There are now only around 7500 tigers left on the planet, although that is well up from the four to five thousand remaining when a major conservation effort, Operation Tiger, was launched in 1972. Sadly, though, the numbers of two races of tiger won't be increasing: the Caspian and Balinese tigers have gone for good.

Nor is the African elephant out of danger. Thanks principally to ivory poaching, only 600,000 now remain – down from several millions at the turn of the century. And if that still seems like a large enough number, remember that it took only fifty years to hunt the North American passenger pigeon, once the commonest bird in existence, to complete and utter extinction. Huge densely packed flocks that could take three days to pass by were reduced to zero: the last passenger pigeon to be seen in the wild was shot on 24 March 1900, and fourteen years later the last representative of the species died in Cincinnati Zoo.

The loss of heritage is certainly sad, but the consequences may be more serious. A species gone is a species that can no longer be used by mankind. In destroying a tropical forest and exterminating the species that lived there, we throw away the key to the medicine cupboard and foodstore of the future. For example, consider the hitherto unregarded Madagascan rosy periwinkle, which contains two powerful drugs for use against leukaemia and Hodgkin's disease. In 1960, eighty per cent of childhood leukaemia cases were fatal. Now, largely due to this plant, eighty per cent of the children survive rather than die. On the other side of the continent, it has been found that West Africa's serendipity berry contains a substance 3000 times sweeter than sugar – but with fewer calories.

Many of our every day agricultural animals and crops have actually been bred from species found in the wild: in their present day form they have never existed as such in the wild. Cattle, pigs, poultry, rice, wheat, maize – they are all produced from a cocktail of genes brought in from the wild. New breeding techniques – as well as the fast developing science of genetic engineering – are constantly refining that cocktail. Better drought resistance? Let's find a still wild cousin that displays the characteristic that we are seeking. Resistance to such-and-such a disease? Let's see now, this natural relative doesn't seem to suffer from it at all. Nor is this pie in the sky. Scientists recently discovered, in a small patch of cloud forest in Mexico, a wild relative of the maize plant – which of course was first found in Central America. It seems to be resistant to four of the eight major maize diseases that plant breeders have been unable to find a solution to. Transferring the genes that provide this resistance into commercial varieties could produce savings of $500 million. Intriguingly, the plant is also a perennial – and capable of growing in cooler and wetter conditions than maize can normally tolerate. These discoveries were made just in time, as the forest where the plant was found was scheduled for imminent destruction.

How many such unique sources *have* been lost, though? No one knows – but by reducing the gene pool from which breeders

9

and scientists can choose, we are deliberately handicapping our ability to produce better yielding, more prolific and hardier food crops and domestic animals. A moment's thought about the fast growing population that they have to serve, and the potentially vastly different climatic conditions that they will have to endure – thanks to factors such as the greenhouse effect and the depletion of the ozone layer – reveals the folly of this. The obscure plants and animals that we are bulldozing out of existence today may contain the very genes that we will need in order to survive tomorrow.

Finally, a thought. Much of our domestic poultry has been bred from the wild. The traditional white farmyard geese that my wife and I keep, for example, are believed to have been developed, in pre-Roman days, from the wild Greylag goose. Scarcely 2000 years later, European sailors discovered the large, flightless and unfortunately very trusting dodo on the island of Mauritius in the Indian Ocean. They were promptly hunted for food or sport, and, by about 1680, the last very dodo had been clubbed to death in the name of progress. Today, we can only look at pictures of dodos and speculate about what sort of a domestic fowl they would have made. Given a more sensible approach, we might today be enjoying the Christmas dodo as much as we now enjoy the Christmas goose or turkey.

SUSTAINABLE USE OF THE PLANET'S RESOURCES AND ECOSYSTEMS

If the bus analogy has seemed an appropriate way to discuss the risks and dangers implied by the first two of the Strategy's objectives, no such cavilling is necessary with the third and final objective. Here, pure logic suffices.

The principle is simple. Remember Mr Micawber's famous

dictum on living within one's means? 'Income twenty shillings a year; expenditure nineteen shillings and sixpence – result happiness. Income twenty shillings a year; expenditure twenty shillings and sixpence – result misery'. The same logic applies to earth's resources. Our use of them, in the long run, has to be *sustainable*. Any long term use that is *un*sustainable results in a running down of stocks and therefore steals from future generations. Steal enough, and the very existence of those generations becomes threatened. As a species, our future depends on each generation leaving the world's level of resources 'as we found them'.

The logic is inexorable. Not that the problem is always dumped on future generations – sometimes we steal from ourselves. Fisheries are a good example. The sea has for centuries been a rich source of food, and forms a large part of the staple diet of several of the world's cultures. Although fish supply only about three per cent of the world's average total protein intake, they supply fourteen per cent of the average *animal* protein intake. In some countries, such as Portugal and Japan, they supply a much higher proportion. In the world's richer countries – notably those in North America and Western Europe – fish consumption has increased sharply in recent years as the health impact has become clearer. Fish offers a way of substituting polyunsaturated fat for polysaturated fat with the same net protein intake.

Fish are also arguably a much 'greener' food than animal meat. Cattle need grain – especially with Western-style agriculture – and are inefficient converters of its protein into meat. It takes about ten times as much grain to produce the same net amount of protein if we eat it as meat instead of as grain. A staggering eighty per cent of the entire US grain harvest is fed to livestock – yet millions of people in the Third World live on the edge of starvation. Fish caught in the sea have not consumed grain that could have been eaten more efficiently by humans directly.

Yet the planet's fish stocks are, according to the UN, on the brink of collapse. Overfishing – and bringing in increasingly younger and smaller fish as the net mesh sizes get smaller – are taking out fish faster than they can naturally replace themselves. The total catch is now running at about ninety million tonnes a year – a figure that must soon surely plummet as the fish simply won't be there to haul in. Even within the UK, a number of formerly rich regional fisheries have been fished to exhaustion. The traditional West Country pilchard industry died years ago, fished out at the end of the last century. Watchmen would stand on towers like the one at Newquay harbour, waiting for the great red stain spreading over the sea that signified the arrival of a pilchard shoal. Boats would set sail immediately, and with whistles and beating oars drive the fish inshore to the beach, where they would be hauled in by their millions, pressed, salted, barrelled and sent inland. Today, only the towers remain.

Like many other green issues, the conservation of fish stocks seem to be honoured more in the breach than the observance. Various schemes have been mooted and tried – the latest UK device being a limit on the number of 'fishing days' that each boat can set sail on. The EC as a whole has both a quota scheme and a policy of buying up and scrapping fishing boats to take them out of the equation. Yet worldwide action is needed. The planet's fish stocks are not an inexhaustible free supply than can be exploited at will, but a finite – and renewable – resource that should be husbanded and managed at a level which is sustainable. This sustainable level, in the long term, will be the one that results in the most consistent yield.

The same principle needs extending to other renewable natural resources – timber and so on. Agricultural land, vital for feeding the world's growing population, is also a renewable resource (although on a longer timescale) that is under threat. An area about the size of China and India combined has suffered 'moderate to extreme' soil degradation in the last forty-five years, according to a recent UNEP study. Deforestation, over-grazing and inappropriate agricultural activities claim a further twenty-four billion tonnes of it each year – washed or blown away, leaving only the rock and subsoil behind. Although the planet's population grows apace, it is reckoned that its area of fertile cropland reached its limit in 1981. The effects won't be felt for some time yet – there's still forest to clear and grassland to plough up, which are environmentally damaging acts in themselves – but *will* inevitably make them-selves felt. As a species, our 'use' of the planet's soil exceeds that which is sustainable. One day, the piper will have to be paid.

13

But not all the resources of the planet *are* renewable. Oil, coal and gas are extracted; metals and minerals are mined. These are effectively non-renewable. Unlike plants, fish or soil, they cannot be used sustainably in the sense that we understand the word. They can, however, be used sparingly, thus extending their effective 'life'. Clearly, recycling is life-extending. Much metal is already recycled, but far more could be. Less wasteful use also extends the life of the planet's non-renewable resources. While this certainly does apply to the use of metals and minerals, it applies far more so to the use of non-renewable sources of energy. As we will see in Chapter 5, studies have shown that large quantities of these are wasted annually. The third way that non-renewable resources can be used more sparingly is by wherever possible switching their applications over to renewable resources instead. Again, it is non-renewable sources of energy that provide the obvious examples – elec-tricity generated from oil, coal or gas could be also generated from hydroelectric, tidal or wind-powered generators, or saved by more efficient use. The methane leaking from municipal waste dumps as their contents decay could be collected and used as fuel instead of escaping into the atmosphere to add to the greenhouse effect. (This is not 'pie in the sky' – a number of such collection systems are already in operation.) Even substituting wood – sustainably grown and cut, of course – for coal and oil as a heat source helps. Oil, gas and coal are such rich sources of useful chemicals that the simple burning of them is a tragic waste. No use of fossil fuels can ever be really sustainable – but it is only prudent to ensure that what use we do make of them is as economic as possible.

Twenty-twenty hindsight

The 1992 Earth Summit in Rio de Janeiro was for many people the first time that the environment became an issue of world political importance. Thousands of people – politicians, heads of state, civil servants and environmental lobbyists – gathered together under the auspices of the UN to paint a new, greener routemap for the future. Thousands of media people gathered to observe, report and analyse this 'unique event'.

In fact, it wasn't. Precisely twenty years earlier, the Swedish capital of Stockholm had hosted the *first* Earth Summit – the 1972 UN Conference on the Human Environment. It was a much more low-key affair. The Stockholm conference was characterised by the attendance of professional diplomats and junior politicians. In contrast, twenty years on, 130 heads of state attended the Rio conference, reflecting the new prominence given to green issues in their countries.

A number of things had contributed to that prominence. Certainly, by the closing years of the 1980s, green issues fashionable both amongst politicians and their constituents. In the

UK, Margaret Thatcher, the then Prime Minister (and a chemist by training) had done much to awaken the interest of her fellow politicians both at home and abroad. Some countries, notably Germany, had seen environmental concern translated into limited political strength, with the election of green members of parliament.

But the biggest spur to action was the increasing awareness that things were going wrong. The politicians might be slow to react to predictions of disaster around the corner, but could most certainly appreciate the potential vote-losing implications of disasters on their doorstep. There had just been too many of them. Dioxin was just another synthetic chemical until a plant manufacturing it at Seveso, in Italy, exploded in 1976 showering hundreds of square miles with the fallout from a toxic cloud of it. Ten days elapsed before the plant's operators, a subsidiary of Swiss pharmaceutical giant Hoffman-La Roche, publicly admitted this. In 1984, another pesticide factory exploded, this time in Bhopal, India. 3500 people died, some more slowly than others, and tens of thousands injured. The legal ramifications run on, almost ten years later.

15

British politicians have had several reminders that environmental disasters were no respecters of national boundaries. The Liberian registered *Amoco Cadiz* went aground whilst steaming up the English Channel in March 1978, spilling its cargo of just under a quarter of a million tons of crude oil. 130 miles of coastline were smothered – most of them (unfortunately for France) French. Politicians and public alike were shocked at the lack of contingency planning and preparedness had fate (and tides) brought more of the oil to British shores.

A few years later, in 1986, a nuclear reactor exploded thousands of miles away in what was then the Soviet Union.

The 1979 near-explosion at Three Mile Island, in the US state of Pennsylvania, had shown that such things were – in contrast to what had been confidently stated – rather more than theoretical possibilities. The nuclear industry had been saying for years that the odds of a serious incident were so remote that they could effectively be discounted. There was, it was alleged, only a fifty per cent chance of such an event once every 23,000 years. Three Mile Island, coming as it did so early into the planet's development of nuclear energy, started to cause some questioning of the veracity of this statistic.

The questioning effectively came to an end on 26 April 1986, when two massive explosions rocked one of the four reactors in the Chernobyl nuclear complex, eighty miles to the north of Kiev. Radioactive debris was hurled a mile into the sky, and it took ten days to bring the burning reactor core under control. A pall of radiation drifted over Europe, through Scandinavia and into Scotland and Wales. Within two weeks, geiger counters throughout the northern hemisphere were ticking away registering the heightened levels of background radioactivity, even as far away as Washington and Tokyo.

Thirty-two died in the explosion and its immediate aftermath, most of them whilst heroically attempting to put out the fires whilst wearing little more than mackintoshes for protection. But far more people will eventually die – some of them thousands of miles from the disaster site. One US study has estimated that Chernobyl will eventually claim 12,000 Soviet citizens and 21,000 Europeans through radiation induced cancers. But there is considerable uncertainty about figures like this: worldwide, as many as one million people may eventually fall victim. Even five years later, British sheep in certain parts of the UK were still being declared unfit for human consumption because of the levels of radioactive dust on the moors and pastureland on which they grazed.

Official reaction was surprisingly muted. No government wanted to produce, through overzealous criticism, a return to the sort of Soviet isolationism seen in the Cold War era. The wisps of smoke from an emerging Soviet democratic movement could be seen, and the situation was sensitive enough without pouring a bucketful of Western cold water on it. In any event, the US Three Mile Island near-disaster and a radiation leak from a previous British one at Windscale (now Sellafield) in 1957 doubtless prompted thoughts of glasshouses and the wisdom of stone throwing. Nuclear disasters weren't necessarily always going to be Russian – but equally, they weren't only going to happen every 23,000 years. It is as yet still too early to say, but Chernobyl probably marked a turning point in the whole nuclear (and, more broadly, environmental) debate. The public at large had previously tended to be generally unconcerned about nuclear power, taking on trust the soothing views about its safety from those it deemed to be in a better possession of the facts. Chernobyl changed that. In country after country, the voice of Mr and Mrs Average – often in unison with their elected representatives – could be heard querying the wisdom of continued investment in nuclear energy.

17

Many environmental activists, whilst not exactly jumping up and down with glee, couldn't help saying 'We told you so . . .'. Their growing confidence was boosted in March 1989 by yet another oil tanker disaster, this time in Alaska – the worst in US history. The Exxon *Valdez* was outside normal shipping lanes, with the captain absent from the bridge, and ripped itself open on a series of underwater reefs. Fifty million litres of oil escaped to wash ashore on almost 1200 miles of unspoilt coastline, including three national parks and four wildlife refuges. Millions of sea and coastal animals and birds died – including whales, sea otters and bald eagles. Exxon drafted thousands of people in in an attempt to save wildlife and clean up what they could of the spillage, spending over a billion dollars in the process.

The scale of these disasters, coming so soon together, rammed several messages home to both businesses and governments. The first was that disasters *happened*. Working on the principle that they happened somewhere else and to someone else just didn't work – and the bigger and more multinational the corporation, the more likely it would be that it itself *was* that someone else, somewhere else. Bhopal, for example, is thousands of miles away from the company's US headquarters – but the consequences of that fateful afternoon in December 1984 continue to tie the hands of Union Carbide's managers and corporate officers years later. Exxon's cleanup of the Alaska coastline has to date cost over a billion dollars, consumed thousands of man years of managerial effort and embroiled it in over 150 complicated law suits – which, depending upon their eventual outcomes, could add enormously to the total cost.

Governments, too, started to wake up to the risks. With a quarter of a million tonnes of oil washing ashore, it's too late to start thinking about getting some containment booms and oil dispersant chemicals manufactured. It also started to dawn on them that prevention was better than cure. There was less likelihood of having to deal with an environmental disaster if proper regulatory regimes existed to try and prevent them. The last twenty years have seen a spate of environmental legislation – in the UK starting with the 1974 Control of Pollution Act, and in the US with the 1969 creation of the Environmental Protection Agency. Controls have progressively got tighter on both sides of the Atlantic, and – as we shall see in later chapters – look set to get tougher still. Staying clean is getting more and more expensive – but the costs of getting dirty can kill the company.

Companies also started to realise the public relations side of their environmental impact. The 1960s had seen, in both Europe and North America, a shift in the way that companies presented their corporate image. 'Product pushing' was replaced by 'company pushing'. As businesses increasingly moved from making one product (or at most a handful of them) to making perhaps hundreds, it made more and more sense to have advertising sell the company that manufactured the product as much as the product itself. That way, the logic ran, consumers' positive feelings about one product could be made to 'spill over' to other, as yet untried, ones. 'Sell the company' became the message every bit as much as 'sell the product'.

Fine – so long as the company's image stayed good. But the idea had a flipside – and a vicious one. Tarnish the company's image, and the damage extended right across the product range. Exxon's self-flagellation following the *Valdez* disaster in large part recognised that if the company didn't whip itself, public opinion would – only harder. The same logic applied to information dissemination. Seveso, thirteen years earlier, had showed how damaging it could be to be caught engaging in a cover-up. Almost as damaging was to be seen to be grudgingly releasing as little information as possible to a press corps in full cry after the facts. As American politicians have come to discover in sex scandals and the like, taking it on the chin with an early admission and a full disclosure invariably proved to be the better long term option.

But the final spur to the Rio Earth Summit was the sheer weight of factual evidence pointing to the need to do something. At the time of the 1972 conference, it was difficult for environmentalists to do much beyond highlight *possible* consequences arising from trends that were still largely nascent. In the ensuing twenty years, those tentative guesses at consequences firmed up to being either 'probable' or 'definite', for two chief reasons. Firstly, scientists and environmentalists improved the general understanding of the global impact of the changes that were taking place, building computer models and the like to explore their impact. Secondly, the trends themselves accelerated, making it increasingly difficult for sceptics to argue that environmentalists' claims were unduly alarmist.

Britain's *Independent* newspaper brought this home on the day that the Rio Earth Summit opened, with a front page entirely devoted to the changes that had taken place in the twenty years since Stockholm to ten significant impacts on the environment. Compiled primarily from UN and WWF sources, it made grim reading. In 1972, for example, the earth's population was 3.84 billion; twenty years on, that figure was 5.47 billion, and growing at ninety-five million a year – the size of the planet's entire population at about 1000 BC.

All those extra people are increasingly concentrated in 'mega-cities' containing over ten million inhabitants. There were just three of these in 1972, only one of which was in a developing country. Twenty years later, thirteen cities fell into this category, nine of them in developing countries where the infrastructure is simply unable to support the demands placed upon it. The simple act of just living in Bombay, for example, is equivalent to smoking contained ten cigarettes a day. Only one person in fifty in Bangkok lives in a dwelling that is connected to the sewerage system. Mexico City has 'faecal snow' – wind-borne dried human excrement. In 1972, thirty-eight per cent of the world's population was defined as 'urban'. In 1992, the figure was forty-six per cent – and will almost certainly be fifty per cent by the year 2000.

All these extra people make rapacious demands on the world's resources – and pump out enormous quantities of pollutants. In 1972 there were 250 million motor vehicles on the road, each burning fossil fuel and emitting a variety of gaseous and solid wastes – some of them, like lead and carbon monoxide, toxic. By 1992, this number had shot up to 600 million vehicles, of which 480 million were cars.

In 1972 the planet had just over 100 power-generating nuclear reactors operated by fifteen nations. In 1992 there were 428, operating in thirty-one countries. Deforestation over the twenty years increased from 100,000 square kilometres a year to 170,000. The planet's two million African elephants reduced to 600,000 over the twenty years, largely through the action of ivory poachers. In 1972 there *was* no chlorine induced hole in the atmosphere's ozone layer, and so nobody had bothered to measure the amount of chlorine in the air. They do now: at just under three parts per billion it is enough to open a hole over the Antarctic each spring. The much thinned ozone layer over Northern Europe (including Britain) did not quite count as a hole in 1992 – but looks set to do so in 1993 or 1994.

21

The atmospheric concentration of carbon dioxide – a contributory factor to the greenhouse effect – stood at 327 parts per million, with sixteen billion tonnes of the gas being released into the air each year. (Some of it, of course, to be turned 'recycled' into oxygen and carbon by the photosynthesising action of plants.) Twenty years on, twenty-three billion tonnes were being released each year, and the concentration had risen to 356 parts per million – clear evidence that nature's photosynthesising couldn't keep pace.

Whatever next?

Where will it all lead? Some predictions are harder to make than others. Useful speculation about the consequences of another Chernobyl, for instance, really relies upon first of all knowing both the geographic location and the size of the 'incident', as the nuclear industry calls it. Only a small proportion of the reactor fuel in just one of Chernobyl's four units was released into the air. Clearly, the next such incident (and it *is* a 'when' rather than an 'if', in the view of many people) could be a lot worse . . . or a lot less severe. We just don't know.

It is also difficult to add any more to what has been said earlier about the consequences of lost biodiversity or the loss of non-renewable resources. The consequences *are* severe – but are 'one offs' rather than a gradually increasing phenomenon we can track over time or plot on a graph. At the time of writing, the numbers of tigers and elephants are once again increasing. Their species may die out – or they may not. It is difficult to tell, and impossible to put a time-based prediction to. Likewise with fossil fuels and other non-renewable resources – there are simply too many imponderables. Modelling can help here, and

22

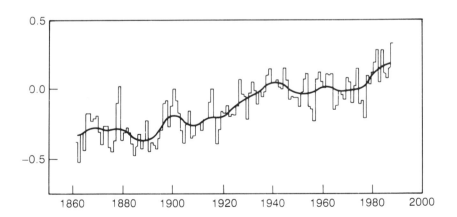

Figure 1.1 The rising trend of global mean temperatures, measured as deviations from the average for 1940 to 1960. In spite of large fluctuations from year to year, the average over successive five-year intervals (smooth curve) shows an increase of about 0.5°C over the past hundred years
(Source: P. D. Jones, CRU, University of East Anglia).

models – for example, of the greenhouse effect or ozone depletion – are becoming increasingly useful in making predictions. While we have come a long way in twenty years, the ball is still moving too quickly for us to be able to tell where – and when – it will land. But we know it will land, and there are many precautions that we can take before it does.

Only where man's activities impact upon climate change through the greenhouse effect are time-based predictions really becoming clear. Figure 1.1 plots the increase in the average global temperature since 1860.

There are of course a number of other factors at work – the eleven year sunspot cycle, 'wobbles' in the earth's orbit and the like – whose impact on global temperatures is as yet somewhat imprecise. Nevertheless, you don't have to be an Einstein to see a steadily increasing global temperature. The earth is clearly getting warmer.

23

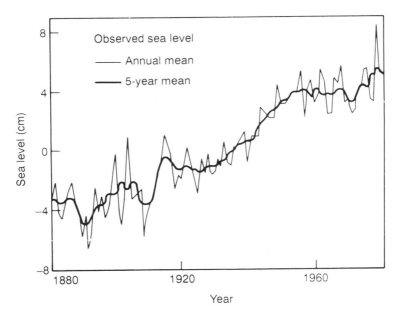

Figure 1.2 The rising trend of global sea level closely follows the rising temperature trend.
(Source: James Hansen/GISS).

A moment's thought reveals that large areas of the globe are ice bound – the poles, northern Canada, Greenland, Siberia and so on. Figure 1.2 tracks the rising temperature against measured sea levels since 1880. The correlation *is* there: the world is getting warmer, the ice caps melt, and the seas rise. This particular graph, incidently, hails originally from US environmental scientist James Hansen – the man whose testimony to Congress so famously convinced British Prime Minister Margaret Thatcher when she read it.

Again, it must be stressed that these figures are far from precise, but scientists are currently estimating that the sea level will have risen by one metre by the end of the twenty first century. At first sight, that doesn't look very much – but how worrying that one metre is depends very much (quite literally) upon where you stand. Vast numbers of people live close to sea level. A one metre rise would submerge eleven per cent of Bangladesh's agricultural land area, for example. A rise of only *half* that much – a mere fifty centimetres – and a land area currently home to sixteen per cent of Egypt's population would sink beneath the waves. The Maldive Islands would more or less vanish completely – the highest point in the entire island chain is less than six foot above sea level.

Nor are the problems solely confined to the Third World. What price London's tidal defense – or Holland's, for that matter? Raise the sea level by a metre, and the 'designed in' odds against them being breached shrink dramatically.

The complex interactions of climate and ocean are only barely understood. Nevertheless, based on research by a wide variety of agencies such as NASA, the Intergovernmental Panel on Climate Change (IPCC), and the UN, some predictions are possible:

■ By the year 2000, global sea levels will have risen between 5 cm and 10 cm, and global temperatures by between 0.1 and 0.2 degrees centigrade – and there could be serious droughts in semi-arid regions.

■ Hurricanes (which already kill thousands of people when they hit areas like Bangladesh) could become much more frequent and severe. The temperate northern latitudes – much of the US, Canada and Europe – can also expect an increase in severe winter blizzards.

■ Some scientists predict that in the next twenty years, wheat yields in the US and Europe will decline by as much as a quarter. Farmers in Scotland, Canada and the former Soviet Union, in contrast, can expect a slight increase. Summer drought will make it difficult to grow traditional crops using conventional techniques in parts of Europe.

25

All of these are serious consequences. Others, perhaps suspected but as yet unconfirmed will doubtless soon become apparent, just as others will come as unpleasant surprises. This is a journey into largely uncharted waters.

And this is just *one* manifestation of the environmental damage that is happening to our planet. It just happens to be the one that, at the moment, it is easiest to chart. We already know that the earth of tomorrow will be hotter, with less fertile land and suffering from more climatic extremes. What we don't know are the answers to slightly vaguer questions such as how much of its waters will be polluted – and by what – or which species will still exist on it, or how much radioactive desert there will be and where.

We do know, though, that the way it's going at present we're making the sort of planet that none of us really wish to live on. Let's now turn to see how businesses can play their part in helping to prevent it from coming into being.

Business and the environment

We now turn to look at the part played by business. This chapter covers:

- **business's role and responsibilities – as a supplier, customer and operator of potentially environmentally-unfriendly plants and processes**

- **the gathering weight of environmental legislation – laws in place now and around the corner**

- **going green – need it cost the earth?**

- **'environmentalism for free' – such as recycling, waste reduction, returnable packaging and energy efficiency**

- **going green as a competitive issue**

- **where management fits in.**

27

Getting down to business

Let's start to look at how businesses can help to play their part in preventing environmental damage by thinking for a moment about the part that they play in contributing to it in the first place. There are really three types of entity that harm the planet's environment:

- governments and government controlled bodies – for example, the civil service, local government and the military

- commercial businesses – power, water and transport

utilities, manufacturers, shops, distribution companies and so on

■ ordinary individuals.

Most environmental damage comes from the first two types of activity – government and commercial businesses. Although ordinary individuals – you and me – may work for the commercial and state bodies (and indeed may actually own commercial businesses such as shops and factories), they don't, in themselves, operate chemical plants, power stations or transport utilities and the like. They may be closely associated with those who do operate them – as shareholders, directors, employees or customers – but the direct environmental impact, strictly speaking, normally comes from the legally incorporated body, rather than from individual people.

There's also considerable ambiguity in the theoretical distinction between government bodies and straightforward commercial activities. Some government bodies are indeed difficult to differentiate from normal businesses in every respect other than that of strict legal ownership. Take two aircraft parked side by side at an airport, for example. One is operated by a state-owned enterprise; the other is flown by a private company. In virtually every respect, they are identical operations, and come under the 'business' heading. Others clearly do not: a government-controlled nuclear research laboratory, is probably more sensibly considered as a branch of the civil service than a state-owned airline or railway company is. Government activities that are largely bureaucratic further confuse matters: again, in terms of the activities undertaken there may be virtually no difference between the government department on one floor of an office block and (say) the insurance company or stockbroker on the floor below them. Both comprise people in a typical office environment, with all the normal office paraphernalia such as computers, coffee machines and photocopiers around them. To a slightly lesser extent, the same goes for educational activities.

The purpose of saying all this is to make the point that the role played by 'business' is indeed an extremely significant one. Business's role – broadly defined – is far larger than that of the individuals who are its ultimate end users, customers or beneficiaries. One external individual, no matter how environmentally committed, has far less influence over an organisation's environmental impact than one of its own managers or employees does. An outside pressure group or individual complaining about the adverse environmental impact of a business's activities or products is often (unfortunately) seen as a nuisance or even as a threat. The instinctive response, more often than not, has usually been to close ranks and refuse to budge – hence the growing weight of environmental legislation that has been enacted to give such complainants the force of law behind them. Yet it might have only taken the action of one committed employee to achieve the required change with no residual sense of pressure or compulsion.

Customers can have even more influence. Returning for a moment to the issue of government versus ordinary commercial bodies, it is perhaps the issue of market forces that provides the best indicator of how 'business-like' an organisation or agency is. Businesses exist to make money: without profits they wouldn't survive – or at least not for very long. For there to be profits, there have to be customers. And in the long run the happier the customers, the higher the profits. So customers have a very powerful voice indeed – especially when they are businesses themselves. It's the point about ordinary individuals, again. One person complaining about a product's packaging is a voice in isolation. The supermarket chain that buys a quarter of the annual output from a particular factory, however, is a voice that is not only listened to but acted on. Many businesses sell to other businesses rather than to end consumers: so people working in offices and factories have the power to change things not only in their own organisation, but in other businesses as well. In fact, most of us are far more powerful influences for environmental good as employees rather than as private individuals. As 'green consumers' we play an important role in preserving the environment – but as green employees, managers and shareholders we can play an even bigger one.

That, in essence, is one of the prime objectives of this book: making people aware of this power, and providing them the facts, arguments and options that they need in order to play their part. Given a bit of determination, getting the office switched over to recycled paper or low energy lightbulbs is within the reach of virtually anyone. Bigger changes – or changes requiring action by suppliers, or a business's own customers – may take longer, but such is the general groundswell of opinion behind environmental issues these days that it's still very much the case that few proposed changes will be met by a flat refusal. Presented with a viable alternative to something that is undeniably having an adverse impact on the environment, most business decision makers will opt for the green alternative if they can. They may not do it for 'green' reasons – but they'll do it.

In fact, one of this book's central arguments is that although it would certainly be nice if people *did* change their policies and practices solely for environmental ethical considerations (as indeed used to be the case), it is by no means necessary for them to do so. There are two other equally powerful arguments in favour of change that are becoming more and more significant as time goes by. The first is the simple rule of law. Environmental legislation is doing much to constrain a business's options in the first place. The second is cost: polluting the environment is expensive – partly because of the penalties arising from the new environmental legislation, and partly because pricing generally is starting to reflect real costs. Recycling anything was never much of an option when plentiful and cheap supplies of the virgin raw material were close at hand – be it power, paper or petroleum. Irrespective of the impact of legislation or public opinion, if going green costs less than not going green, businesses will switch.

Don't call us, we'll call you

Let's look first at the effect that environmental legislation is having – and, more importantly, that it is likely to have in the future. The midnight knock on the door from the 'Green Police' is some time away, but there's no doubt that the authorities are increasingly vested with stronger and stronger powers, and are becoming quicker to react to the activities of violators. The whole character of environmental legislation has changed substantially over the last quarter century or so. At the time of the Industrial Revolution, for example, when mankind's activities first started to impact on the planet's environment, applicable legislation of any kind was completely lacking.

Mill, mine and factory owners had few legal strictures placed upon them. When such legislation did start to appear, it largely related to what we would now term health and safety issues – firstly to direct injuries to employees, and secondly to customers and surrounding residents. Environmental damage was proscribed only when it directly harmed humans, and not when it directly harmed the environment but only *in*directly harmed people. The whole ethos has now changed: activities directly injurious to people continue to be unlawful, but so – increasingly – are activities that are only indirectly harmful. Only the degree of 'indirectness' differs. The pollution of the sea, land and atmosphere is outlawed – but so, in Germany at least, is the use of non-returnable 'secondary' product packaging. The degree of directness is clearly far greater in the first instance than the second: the concept of 'harm' has evolved from being one of specific acts harmful to people in the short term to one of a rather vaguer and less precise damage to the environment in general.

The following is a list of some of the legislation currently enacted in the UK (or more precisely, in England and Wales) at the time of writing – Autumn 1992. They all generally have their counterparts in other countries, as well as in a number of overriding EC directives. They are listed here as *examples* of the type of legislation that businesses are subject to.

32

- The Environmental Protection Act 1990

- Control of Substances Hazardous to Health Regulations 1988

- The Control of Pollution Act 1974

- The Food and Environmental Protection Act 1985

- Notification of Installations Handling Hazardous Substances Regulations 1982

- The Planning (Hazardous Substances) Act 1990

- The Control of Pollution (Special Wastes) Regulations 1980

- The Health and Safety at Work Act 1974

- Control of Industrial Major Accident Hazard Regulations 1984

- The Clean Air Acts of 1956 and 1968

- The Water Resources Act 1991

- The Water Industry Act 1991

- Various EC directives

These are amongst the major pieces of legislation affecting what might be termed the 'average' business. Other, more specific laws and regulations exist, and cover less common businesses, such as those handling nuclear or genetic materials, or transporting hazardous substances by land, air or sea. It is also worth pointing out that the provenance of some of the legislation listed above owes much to learning by experience. The Control of Industrial Major Accident Hazard Regulations, for example, came about as a direct result of the Seveso accident referred to in Chapter 1. The Clean Air Act of 1956 came about through concern over the notorious London 'peasouper' smogs – the 1952 one, for example, is estimated to have killed 4000 people.

33

As we will see in subsequent chapters, the overall reach of these pieces of legislation is quite extensive. The uninitiated may well read the list above and think that they are unlikely to be affected, but would be wrong to do so. Simply put, even the burning of office waste in a factory yard is an offence under the Environmental Protection Act. And the burning of *industrial* waste by the same factory is an even greater offence – the actual magnitude being dependent upon the materials being burnt. The Act toughened up and much improved on the provisions contained in previous legislation – primarily the 1974 Control of Pollution Act – by imposing a duty of care on all of those involved in both the disposal *and* the original production of waste in the first place. Criminal sanctions apply for a breach of this duty; fines are unlimited, and offenders are also liable for two years' imprisonment. Pollution – and any form of environmental damage covered by existing law – is a serious matter, and not one that businesses can get around by paying lip service to. The oil company Shell, for example, was fined £1 million for polluting the river Mersey. Interestingly, the judge said that the fine would have been higher had the company not been so involved in socially responsible initiatives.

The extent to which the ultimate sanction of imprisonment will curtail the worst excesses is as yet unclear, but there seems little doubt that directors and senior managers are (perhaps slowly) waking up to the unpleasant reality that the laxness that they might have historically condoned could – quite literally in some cases – blow up in their faces, resulting in them personally facing prosecution and imprisonment. Fining the company is one thing, but being jailed is quite another. Managements that have historically turned a blind eye to matters such as waste disposal, because of the potential cost of 'doing it properly', now have a more personally pressing need to act in a responsible manner. Yet, as we will see, irrespective of any legislation, the idea that polluting was somehow a cheaper option is already looking outdated, and likely to rapidly become more so.

Waste not, want not

Environmental writers and activists sometimes give the impression that waste recycling is something that businesses need persuading about. Nothing could be further from the truth. As virtually anyone who works in industry knows, most companies have some processes where they recycle their own raw material wastes and byproducts back into their products. Trimmings, off-cuts, not-quite-up-to-spec materials and so on are all regarded with a view to going back into the process for either straightforward rework or absorption into lower grade materials. Raw materials usually represent too high a cost in relation to prevailing profit margins for companies to overlook opportunities to make sure that every ounce of input is matched by a corresponding output.

So the idea of recycling – in this form, anyway – isn't new. Profit-conscious businesspeople have been doing it for ages. Not only does it help reduce the need to purchase raw materials, but it also cuts down on the amount of waste that needs to be taken away and disposed of – all of it taken away at a cost, of course. Environmental activists who assume that industry is either deaf or indifferent to their pleas are simply ill informed. The concept is well understood and there is no complacent cadre of wanton wasters to be won over. People who haven't been inside a factory in their lives need to start replacing their prejudices with a few facts.

35

There are, however, two opportunities for business to do more – and, again, not at a cost but to increase profits. The first of these lies chiefly in simply extending, in effect, what the factory or business considers as 'its' waste. At the moment, it is waste material arising within the manufacturing process that is recycled. What the activists are seeking is the reclaiming of waste materials arising *after* manufacture – the so-called 'post-consumer' waste. Chapter 4 looks in detail at this, but the problem is essentially one of logistics and organisation rather than technology or will.

As anyone who has consciously tried – as a *business* buyer – to purchase genuinely recycled materials will confirm, it's not easy. Companies' sales departments are more geared up to dealing with customers' questions on price, quality and delivery than they are to cope with questions about recycled content and the like. Not only is the information not there, but it's difficult to find the materials. The flow of materials back towards the factory gate just isn't yet big enough. 'Raw materials' still essentially means *virgin* raw materials.

The process of extending the material supply chain out towards the consumer, rather than backwards to the planet's resources *is* however slowly taking place. Too often, though, it's seen as a soul salving piece of environmental activism rather than simple business good sense. Supermarket chains, for example, already collect and return for reprocessing much of the paper and plastic packaging that the goods that they sell arrive in. This occasionally verges on the absurd – one large supermarket chain insists that the recycled plastic products that it sells contain only recycled plastics from its stores and no one else's! Clearly, a truly thought-out green policy would not do this. Nevertheless, by setting up a flow of plastics for recycling, the supermarket chain has ensured that everyone benefits. There's the satisfaction of being green of course, but also lower prices to the consumer, as well as higher profits for the store and the manufacturer. Recycled plastic is both cheaper than virgin plastic (which is made from non-renewable oil, of course) and more stable in price.

Many supermarkets increasingly have collection points in their car parks for the newspapers, cans and glass that consumers bring back. In theory, as we will see, a lot of waste – provided that it can be collected and sorted – can be used by someone, somewhere in place of a virgin raw material.

Business's role lies not in changing its mindset from one of obstinate refusal to consider the recycling option, but in encouraging the formation of the organisational chain that will bring the recyclable wastes to its doorstep. Historically, it has always been easier to go and procure virgin raw materials from nature, because that is where they have been found in the greatest quantity and at the highest concentration. It simply

36

wasn't sensible to consider using a relativity few aluminium cans (say) when the quantity of aluminium that was required was several thousand tonnes. It was easier to buy from an established supply chain that started with mined bauxite ore and then refine it.

Given the appropriate collection channels, though, returned cans become available in a quantity sufficient to become usable. What's more, the metal that they comprise is already refined; there's no need to process hundreds of tonnes of ore to get a handful of tonnes of aluminium – once refined, recycling is virtually a tonne for tonne exchange, and one with significantly lower energy costs. In fact, the production costs of recycled aluminium are only five per cent of those involved in producing from mined ore.

The same logic goes for glass, plastics, metals and paper – and the average reader should be able to confirm with a moment's thought and perhaps a quick glance around them how significant a proportion of industrial output either contains or falls wholly into those four categories. Markets on a more or less structured basis for these have been around a long time – the traditional 'rag and bone' man with his horse and cart may be a thing of the past but scrap metal and waste paper merchants appear in virtually every phone book in the land. Glass and plastics recyclers are less common, but can still be found. The act of sending scrap and waste materials to these recyclers not only helps boost the supply to meaningful levels, but cuts down on business's own waste disposal costs. If businesses work on the premise that somebody, somewhere recycles what is being thrown away, it should provide them both a short term boost to profits through lower disposal costs as well as a longer term cost reduction through helping build up the supply of genuine recycled materials.

The second opportunity for business to do more recycling is a more controversial one, although again one that is far from a new idea. The basic idea behind it is very simple. When people discard consumer durables (or semi-durables) it is usually *not* because the whole item has worn out or contains nothing of salvageable use. It is more usually the case that although one or two key components may have worn out or broken, the remainder are in fine working order, with plenty of theoretical life left in them.

The motor industry has long made use of this. 'Exchange' parts are commonly sold as spares – bring in your broken carburettor, alternator or whatever and exchange it for a reconditioned refurbished one. Some of the components in the exchange part *are* new, but most are enjoying a second, third or subsequent lease of life. Clearly, for example, components like carburettor outer bodies cannot in any meaningful sense 'wear out' at all – it is only a handful of inner bits and pieces like diaphragms and jets that move or experience wear.

But at the time of writing, it is German motor manufacturers who are extending this idea to its logical conclusion and regarding the whole vehicle as returnable. Partly prompted by strict German environmental laws, and partly for their own ethical, marketing and manufacturing considerations, BMW and Mercedes-Benz have been working hard to make the recycling of more and more of their vehicles as practical a consideration as possible. This involves more than just recycling in the sense of incorporating returned components in exchange gearboxes and carburettors and the like. It also means recycling the material that components are made of, if recycling the component itself is not a practical proposition. A plastic moulded bumper, for example, cannot sensibly be recycled whole – there are just too many dents and scratches on it – but the plastic that it is made of can be re-moulded to form either a new bumper or some other entirely different component.

There are all sorts of practical problems with this. Taking just plastics, for example, there are an awful lot of different types of plastic on a car. Each has been chosen for reasons of initial cost or suitability for the job – *not* because of its suitability for recycling. The sheer number of types of plastic makes recycling them difficult – the plastic that makes a door handle, for example, may or may not be suitable for use as a steering wheel. Efforts have to be made to reduce the number of plastics to a smaller number of more easily recyclable ones.

Efforts also have to be made to improve the flow of parts back. Scrap yards have historically 'recycled' car parts for a long time, enabling people to buy secondhand parts before what's left is compressed in a crusher and melted down for its metal content – during which the residual plastics and fabrics simply vaporise off into the atmosphere. A more intelligent form of recycling requires a flow of cars back to a central point where the various types of plastic and metal – steel, copper, aluminium and so on – can be properly separated out for subsequent re-use. It's back to the question of logistics and organisation that we looked at earlier. Again, German law is likely to be the first to make this mandatory, with a law under consideration that would require – perhaps by the mid-1990s – manufacturers to take back their vehicles at the end of their lives and disassemble them.

39

Nor are such moves confined to the motor industry. In electronics, for example, Hewlett-Packard issue pre-paid postage labels with their laser printer toner cartridges for people to post back their empty ones for re-filling and resale.

And there is a lot more, the experts say, that *could* be recycled or re-used if manufacturers found it piled up on their doorsteps waiting to be actioned. Predictably, though, hands are being raised in horror as manufacturers point to the costs and complications of it all. This is somewhat disingenuous – manufacturers have pointed to the costs and complications of all sorts of new ideas and legislation since time immemorial. Victorian factory owners fought tooth and nail against basic laws governing child labour, sweatshops and unsafe working conditions. The trick is to recognise either the intrinsic benefits of something – even if it means change and upheaval – or its ultimate inevitability. While there would indeed be a cost to returning more scrapped durables to their manufacturers for re-use or recycling, given the right amount of organisation and effort, it would probably work quite smoothly. The hand wringing is more about setting the system up than using it once it is in place.

As we will see in Chapter 4, it is easy to come to the conclusion that the supposed costs of such schemes are too high. Critics tend to lump in the one-off costs of establishing the backwards flow of old parts in the first place, for example, forgetting that they have in effect already had to 'pay' for the system that at present already brings them virgin materials from half way around the world. Absurdly, the tax regime in some countries actually favours the use of virgin raw materials – wood pulp being a case in point. The key issue that is often overlooked is that few businesses themselves have actually said 'if we *could* get our old products back, what could we do with them? And what would we need to help us do it more efficiently?'

For the issue at hand is not purely to match or reduce the unit product cost, but to turn from a culture that makes profligate use of resources that will one day dry up, into one that husbands those resources sensibly – even if it *does* mean a slight increase in costs. The critics who argue against the description of the costs as 'slight' are simply misinformed – and for two reasons. Firstly, it is a nonsense to view non-renewable resources as infinite – and how do you evaluate the cost of a plastic component in the future, when the oil to make it from has all gone? It's the old schoolchild's problem of comparing apples and oranges: labour and organisational costs now versus raw material costs in the future. And secondly, little thought has actually gone into setting up such operations. Although returnable bottles have worked in certain drinks sectors, there are few other precedents. Bottles in any case are very simple to clean and re-use. What does one do with a car, or computer or washing machine? Manufacturing industry has concentrated for decades on more and more efficient ways of *assembling* things. No one has really tasked bright engineers to come up with better and better ways of taking things apart for re-use. We have assembly machines by the million – but where are the *dis*assembly machines? The critics who argue that the concept is unworkable simply haven't tried to make it work.

But those businesses that attempt – Canute-like – to hold back   41
the future will fail. The argument that the smart thing to do is keeping one's head down and waiting for the public to latch onto something else instead misses the mark by a mile. It didn't work with slavery, it didn't work with Dickensian employment and safety conditions and it won't work with the environment.

Oddly enough, American businesses seem to be more amenable to this than British or other European ones. As recently as the 1960s, many of them were very actively (albeit unthinkingly) discriminating against blacks and women. This was only natural – much as they would like to have promoted an able woman or black, the people reporting to these individuals 'wouldn't have liked it'. The easiest course was to find an excuse and promote – or hire – another white male.

Yet laws came in to change all this. Schoolchildren were bussed to different schools. White males found themselves reporting to women or blacks, or working as equals to them. The world, it seemed, didn't stop.

Nor will it, one guesses, with the environmental laws that are coming. Businesses can protest as loudly as they can about their unwillingness to take back old cars for recycling, but if it's a choice between that and going out of business, there are no prizes for guessing which way they'll jump. And it won't make a jot of difference to competition, as all firms will be affected – except in one small but vital way. As with other aspects of environmental change, the question of timing is important. The costs, difficulties and drawbacks associated with the change will undoubtedly be greater for businesses that leave it until the last minute.

Going green as a competitive issue

From what we've seen so far, it's clear that there are half a dozen or so major environmentally driven changes coming along to the way that businesses in general operate. The 'green movement', if we can call it that, is not some passing enthusiasm that will soon wane and die away, allowing things to revert to what they were. The environmental dangers facing the planet are serious ones, and ones that governments, pressure groups and individuals are not going to ignore. Businesses are therefore in it for the long haul – just as with the other socially-driven changes to working practices and employment conditions that they have had to make over the years. The clock has never turned back on these issues, nor will it with environmental ones.

The important difference today, though, is that while the pressure of change on business's working practices and employment conditions has slowed down – the dark, satanic mills of yesteryear now being found only in history books and heritage centres – the pace of green change is accelerating. The half dozen or so major elements of this pressure of change can be simply expressed.

- Manufacturing processes have to become greener – more efficient, less energy-intensive and using and producing fewer environmentally unfriendly chemicals and materials.

- Products themselves are coming under increasing environmental scrutiny – so no CFCs, raw materials from endangered species or wasteful use of resources.

- Waste is an emerging issue – controls on what can be disposed of where are becoming tighter, and the actual cost of disposal is rising sharply as landfills become scarcer and legislation forces waste disposal operators' practices under an increasingly critical spotlight.

- Waste of all sort can be cut down if products – or parts of them – can be recycled. 'Recyclability' is going to become less and less of an option and more of a legislatively imposed requirement.

43

- Greener utilisation of both renewable and non-renewable resources in general will become of increased concern to both customers and employees. Pressures will mount for businesses to operate in an 'environmentally neutral' a way as possible – perceived non-green activities such as conspicuous consumption of energy or other resources will become a competitive 'drag factor'.

- Legislation will increasingly bear an EC imprimatur. Most environmental legislation at present is of national origin – businesses in France obey one set of laws, businesses in the UK another. Over the next few years, legislation emanating from Brussels will increasingly override much of this national regulation. It is far too early to say what the detail of that Brussels-inspired legislation will comprise, but from the shape of the EC directives already in force and in the draft stage, it seems likely that they will represent a much tougher green regime than UK firms face at present. In particular, experts believe that harmonisation will bring into UK law an extension of the 'polluter pays' principle, and a 'no fault' liability for damage to the environment – a concept that already exists in some EC countries such as Belgium, Germany and Italy, but not in the UK. What this means is that businesses will be held directly responsible for pollution, even if – as under UK law at the moment – they themselves were not strictly at fault.

So, like it or not, businesses will have to change. Smart businesses will start to do so now, enabling them to make the required changes at their own pace, and without incurring the costs of last minute panic measures. There are a number of reasons for this. Although many of the changes that will be necessary can be made relatively quickly, they still need thinking through properly in order to be as effective and economic as possible. There's no point changing something once and then changing it again because it wasn't properly thought through the first time. To take a relatively trivial example, suppose a business decides to move away from using plastic cups in its canteen and vending machines, and switches to a different type of vending machine using paper cups instead. Fine – until someone points out that the paper cups are wax coated, and therefore still use non-renewable oil. Changing schemes once more, this time to a 'bring your own mugs and wash them up afterwards' catering system, consumes management time and company money once again. A little thought at the beginning can pay dividends later on.

More seriously, though, some decisions cannot be rushed – the survival of the business itself may be at stake. If a company's products or processes have to become greener, for example, it can take months or years to develop and test alternatives. Replacing chemical compound x with chemical compound y may make significant differences to product performance, longevity or production cost – none of which might be apparent at first. The costs of bodging the job and having to make yet another change, to chemical z, are considerable – and may not be solely financial in nature. Angry customers, lost orders and slipped market share can be difficult to attribute precise numbers to, but do eventually work their way through to a lower profit.

Plant and machinery considerations are important, too. Although equipment lives generally are becoming shorter, managers still – outside particularly fast evolving industries such as electronics – look for useful lives of ten years or so from the fixed investments that they make. They may well charge depreciation to their accounts over a shorter period, but would be disappointed (to say the least) if their spanking new machinery became redundant or needed expensive refits after only four or five years. Ironically, that is the risk being run by managers who fail to plug the 'green factor' into their investment equations. Production processes quite legal now may well be outlawed completely under (say) new EC-inspired anti-pollution legislation for example – leaving manufacturers to scrap or modify existing plant as best as they can.

45

And waste disposal is not only becoming more strictly controlled, but more costly. Managers need to start thinking now about how they can cut down on the waste and effluents produced by their businesses. Careful planning now can prevent costly process changes and product reformulations later – as well as last-minute desperate searches for a waste disposal contractor to take stuff away at any cost. And it's not just factories that have some navel-gazing to do either. Offices and shops generate an awful lot of paper and plastic waste. The straightforward disposal of these into landfill sites is going to become a costlier and costlier exercise. Recycling – or better still, a reduction in the quantity of waste being generated – will become a financial concern as well as a green one.

The manager's role

So if businesses have a role to play, which of the various stakeholders in an enterprise – owners, employees, managers and so on – have the largest contribution to make? Contrary to the beliefs of some in the green camp, it is usually *not* the 'owners'.

Owners are rarely the despotic rabidly anti-green polluters that some of the more extreme green literature paints them as being. In all but the smallest of businesses, in fact, owners rarely have the opportunity to act in a malignant way – they simply aren't close enough. The vast majority of owners of significantly sized businesses are holders of publicly quoted shares – you and me, either directly or indirectly through the institutions administering our pensions and insurance policies. Although *in theory* shareholders exert absolute control over their company, in practice a single shareholder has very little power. As those with shares in one of the privatisations of the 1980s will recognise, even a committed direct shareholder who actually attended company annual meetings would find that the influence that they could exert in practice in fact was fairly minimal.

Nor does the average employee have much influence beyond 'whistle blowing' to their superiors – or the outside world. The more senior an employee, the greater the authority vested in them, certainly, but in practical terms only a relative handful of staff – the managers – can make significant decisions affecting a business's environmental policies and practices. So much of

46

this book is accordingly aimed at management. Unlike owners, who have authority but not information to act upon, and ordinary employees, who might have information but no authority, management have both. They can know what needs to be done, and also have the wherewithal to do it. Before this, though, they need to find out what's wrong – if anything – in the first place. This is the purpose of the 'environmental audit', which examines a business to see how green its policies and practices really are. Let's now turn to Chapter 3, to look at undertaking an environmental audit – how to go about organising one, what to look for, and how to determine the priorities for action.

47

Carrying out an environmental audit

In this chapter, we look at:

- **what environmental audits are**

- **the audit approach used in this book, and how it ties in with each of the following chapters**

- **planning the audit and carrying it out.**

Not just a greenwash

The term 'environmental audit' has a nice catchy sort of feel to it. Why, a management can get a virtuous glow just from thinking about it – not to mention the fact that it's excellent public relations. Bung in a few low energy lightbulbs or something and get back to business as usual.

But environmental audits have to be more than mere tokens if they are to produce serious results. Otherwise, they *will* be just vehicles for a spot of cheap PR and a sop to any activists and will soon be discredited. Managements shouldn't regard the fact that there is as yet no statutory definition of what comprises an environmental audit – unlike, say a financial audit – as an excuse to simply whitewash over any facts that seem too unpalatable or too expensive to do anything about. There's no point accepting the logic of the previous chapters – that something has to be done, both for the planet's survival as well as the company's own long-term competitive viability – and then paying only superficial lip service to the process that actually delivers that change.

And although there isn't as yet a codified environmental audit as such, the experts have broadly identified the sort of approach that generally produces the best results. Whilst each expert and auditing body has their own version of this generic audit – incorporating their own particular views and visions – the 'mainstream' audit generally goes through the stages in the diagram below:

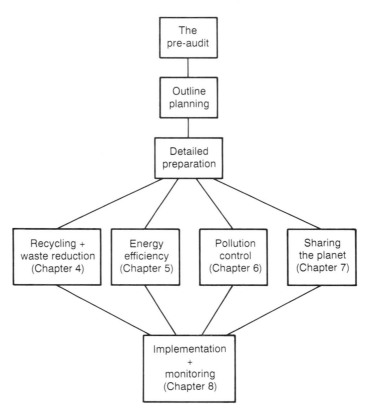

Figure 3.1 Stages of the 'mainstream' audit.

The rest of this book traces through this overall format. The present chapter deals with the issues surrounding the planning and initial organisation of the audit – the 'pre-audit' stage, and the subsequent Outline Planning and Detailed Preparation stages. We then go on to look, in Chapters 4 to 7, at each of the principal areas of *opportunity* arising from an audit – recycling, improved energy efficiency, pollution control and improving a business's relationship with the creatures and ecosystems that it shares the planet with. Finally, in Chapter 8, we look at the process of implementation – the putting in place of corrective measures where appropriate, how to win the business's staff and stakeholders over to the idea of doing business in a greener way, and of setting up a monitoring mechanism to maintain the environmental momentum that we are going to put in place.

First, though, we look at some basic issues in the planning and administration of an environmental audit. Business people don't need 'selling' on the virtues of a proper organisation and a sensibly formulated plan – we understand that it's planning that all too often differentiates the winners from the losers. Start with a shambles and you'll usually end up with one, too.

But before plunging into looking in detail at the practicalities of issues such as improving energy efficiency and setting up a recycling scheme, we do need to briefly touch on some of the aspects of planning and preparing an environmental audit. The focus isn't on the theory of planning – that's an area that professional managers obviously have a great deal of expertise in already – but on some of the trickier practicalities as they relate to businesses moving into an active consideration of green issues for the first time.

THE PRE-AUDIT

The 'pre-audit' first of all 'scopes' the audit. It may be a long process, or a short one. The principal areas of concern in a business might be already known, or it may be necessary to conduct an investigation to a gather a 'broad brush' impression about what areas should be focused on in the audit proper. In a business unused to thinking in an environmental way, there may be widespread ignorance, and management cannot easily do a sudden about turn and view the operation from a new and greener perspective. A process of self-education, both in terms of the business's operations and their environmental impact, may well be necessary. The pre-audit stage entails a quick scan through the whole business to determine a suitable area (or areas) to come back and look at again in much more detail in the audit proper.

Size of business has an obvious bearing on the complexity and duration of an audit. In a relatively small business, it *is* possible to review the whole operation in one go. In larger organisations, though, a total audit might be virtually impossible, no matter how desirable. A multi-million, multi-site business cannot stop everything and examine itself all in one go – quite apart from the deleterious effect on profits and customers, the outcome would be an enormous mass of indigestible data that would prove difficult for management to get to grips with. A much better solution is to bite off discrete and manageable portions and thoroughly digest the implications of these before moving on. Apart from anything else, it's generally a quicker way to deliver green benefits, too. Rather than take a year on the audit, reviewing everything before implementing anything, changes for the better can be made in a matter of weeks by deliberately restricting the focus.

It's easy for an enthusiastic management team to want to skip the pre-audit stage, in order to get on with the more exciting part of what they see as the 'meat' of the project, but the temptation should be resisted. A proper pre-audit – no matter how brief – will serve as an indispensable route map for the audit as a whole, detailing the areas of the business to be involved, the broad issues to be examined, and the intended timescale for completion.

OUTLINE PLANNING

With the pre-audit complete, it's time to get on with the audit itself. There are several purposes of this first stage of the process. Again, though, they shouldn't be rushed or skimped – a few minutes deliberation at this stage can save literally hours of frustration later on. Although the broad focus of the 'audit area' is understood, there are a number of other things that need deciding and finalising. The first of these is in fact one of the most important aspects of the whole process.

Selecting the review team

53

Audits don't happen on their own – they have to be carried out. But who should do this? There are a number of basic 'do's' and 'don'ts' to consider.

- DO make it a team effort, even if the business (or area of it to be considered) is – in theory, anyway – small enough for one person to carry out. An audit or review carried out by one individual runs the risk of being branded as that person's pet project, and therefore may lack both credibility and support elsewhere in the organisation. A team effort will inevitably have a broader constituency – and will help during the implementation phase.

- DON'T just assemble a group of spare or underutilised people together and tell them to get on with it. If they are the sort of people that can be readily spared, then they probably aren't the right people for the task – unless all you want is a greenwash. Bright, committed people who aren't afraid to ask questions and – if necessary – rock boats, will produce an audit that is worth having. Being 'green' to start with certainly helps in understanding some of the issues, but is in no sense a necessary prerequisite.

■ DO try and make the team as multidisciplinary as possible. This not only serves to broaden its constituency again, and helps the team acquire the support they will need both during the audit and when implementing any actions, but will add to the quality of the findings. Depending on the business and its activities, pure technical expertise may or may not be required in quantity or depth – a chemical plant will obviously have different requirements from a light engineering company or office-based business. In practice, the chief benefit of the multidisciplinary team comes not from the range of technical skills that it embodies, but from the diversity of points of view that it offers. The old adage about two heads being better than one is rarely truer.

■ DO make sure that the team leader is the right individual for the job. They have a critical role to play in the audit, and it is essential that they are up to the task. They will also need to be good managers of both people and projects if an equally old adage – the one about too many cooks spoiling the broth – is not to prove just as true. A strong personality, well known and respected in the organisation, is required. As with the case of the individual team members, these aren't the sort of people who can normally be painlessly spared for a task – but again, if the audit is to actually mean anything, it's not sensible to cut corners or skimp.

■ DO make sure that the team is vested with sufficient authority to overcome any difficulties or obstacles that are found (or are placed) in its path. In practice, this means allocating responsibility for the audit to one of the senior members of the organisation – a director, or equivalent – who

54

can ensure that difficult issues are resolved and that any delays to the planned timescale are minimised.

Outline policy definition

This senior individual will also be influential in formulating the initial policy guidelines that the team will be working to. ('Initial' because they may need revising in the light of the outcome of the audit. It's not unknown for businesses to set out towards environmental goals that are simply unattainable in the short-to- medium term – either because of cost, physical impossibility, or because the business is too far way from being as green as it had at first imagined itself to be. Formulating them first as 'initial' policy guidelines allows some flexibility, should this be required – and without the need for an embarrassing climbdown later on.)

55

Again, managements must resist the temptation to rush in and draw something up along the lines of 'we want to be green'. Overall, the intention should be to try and determine the answers to the following questions. These will then naturally form themselves into a description of how the business sees itself moving towards a greener future – and also, as a useful byproduct, provide the *raison d'être* for that move. Instead of a vague and woolly green direction, there will be a justified – and justifiable – statement of where the business stands in respect to the environment, and in which directions it is moving.

- What is the area to be looked at actually doing? What are the inputs, what are the outputs (including byproducts and wastes), and where do they go?

- Can – and should – this be improved? How environmentally friendly is it? Are there any applicable legislative standards that we should be complying with – either on the statute book now, or likely to be so within our 'decision horizon'? (Which may be as long as a decade, don't forget.)

- Could *more* be done? Irrespective of laws or standards, do we honestly believe that our processes and products are as environmentally-neutral as possible? What are our competitors doing? What is 'best practice'?

- What opportunities are there for cost reduction? Can we recoup or minimise *direct* costs through waste elimination, process improvements, energy efficiency or recycling? And what about *indirect* costs – such as insurance, cost of finance and potential future legal liabilities?

Preparation of outline project plan

Finally, an outline project plan should be prepared and approved. Not too detailed a one – it won't be possible to go into much depth because the nature and scale of so many of the activities are still unknown – but certainly one comprehensive enough to show target timescales and resource requirements for each of the stages of the audit, leading to an overall completion date.

The outline plan performs two primary purposes. Firstly, it serves notice on senior management of what the likely timescales and resource requirements are going to be. There's no point the Board of Directors, having asked for an environ-mental audit, and having assigned one or two people to the team, then expecting an answer to arrive the following week. The outline plan, by throwing up likely timescales and resource costs early on, enables changes to made to either of them before any more serious work gets under way.

Its second purpose is to provide a top-level route map for the team itself. For most members of the team, this will be the first time that they have performed this role, so activity timescales may drift as individuals – or the team as a whole – explore unfamiliar territory. Having some preliminary indication of how long each activity must take prevents things from bogging down as issues are debated and options explored.

DETAILED PREPARATION

Once the overall outline of the audit has been thought through and agreed, it's time to start getting down to business. There are all sorts of questions to be decided. What background legal and environmental material needs to be studied? What sort of information needs to be collected – and how do we go about it? What does the workplan look like – and who in the team is responsible for undertaking which activities? When shall the 'milestone' meetings to review progress be held – both within the team itself and outside it?

57

Review legal and environmental background

The recognition will rapidly dawn that there are big gaps in the business's knowledge about itself. Most of an organisation's information focuses on its outputs rather than its inputs or wastes. The process of information gathering will plug these, some more easily than others, but it is first of all necessary to know what questions to ask. Are any of these chemicals deleterious to the ozone layer? Can you assure us that this wood has not been unstainably harvested? Is this paper or cardboard recycled? What happens to the waste chemicals from process X after the contractor takes them away? And so on.

'Green' literature contains some of the more usually asked questions. Chapters 4, 5 and 6 of this book, for example, cover in detail the areas of recycling, energy efficiency and pollution control. But it is difficult to cater for the circumstances of particular businesses in books and magazines intended for a wider readership. Trade associations and industry journals often provide a better way of homing in on the issues facing particular businesses.

External consultants and advisors can also help (although usually at a price), as can a third – and sometimes overlooked – source, namely the regulatory authorities. These, whilst admittedly there to ensure compliance with the law, do offer advice on alternative methods and techniques for not just meeting the regulatory requirements but also exceeding them. As we shall see, government departments, agencies and other resource providing bodies also offer extensive assistance in their particular areas of expertise. Staff working for (in the UK) local authorities, the Department of Energy, the National Rivers Authority and the electricity companies, for instance, are only a phone call away, yet are considerable repositories of knowledge and advice.

58

Planning the data collection

Contacts with all of these sources of help and information will also be useful when there are actual facts and figures about the business's environmental performance to consider. Discussions about theoretical 'what if's' are fine, but hard data provides a much more useful way of ranging in on particular options and alternatives.

Yet where is this data to come from? It's probably available – or can be got at – but how should it be collected? And what will happen to the data once it is obtained – will it be formally analysed by (say) a computer, or just sifted through by hand? This is again one of those seemingly trivial points that management (or the audit team) can rush past in their headlong enthusiasm to deliver results. Doing so is dangerous, and can throw the whole audit off the rails. Consider some of the complications:

- A business with a lot of suppliers of raw materials (for example, retail and distribution outlets, or electronic assembly plants) clearly needs to seek a lot of information from its suppliers. Questionnaires are useful ways to collect large volumes of data, particularly if the information needs to be 'standardised' for entry into a computer. This can be difficult if the environmental issues vary widely from material to material, or supplier to supplier – or if there is uncertainty as to what might emerge in the answers. Here, face-to-face interviews are the best option. Again, though, a business with many suppliers to conduct interviews with is likely to find the task a lengthy and unwieldy one. A compromise might be to conduct a limited number of face-to-face interviews with a representative cross section of suppliers, considering the issues that emerge, and then going on to construct a standardised questionnaire, perhaps supplemented by telephone interviews.

59

- A business less broadly focused on its supply chain needs to consider its own operations more fully. What information is already kept? How suitable is it for the form of analysis the team intends to undertake? Is it largely numeric in format or mainly qualitative? Are any measurements necessary – of, say, waste gases, liquids or byproducts – and does the business actually possess the necessary equipment with which to make them? If not, can the measurement process be subcontracted out – and if so, to whom?

- Data also needs collecting on the various improvement options that are available. Although there should in theory be only one – 'best practice' – best practice today is not the same as best practice tomorrow, and tomorrow's new technology might be just around the corner. Then again, 'theoretical' best practice might simply be too expensive – because of either limitations in the technology or the business's finances. As we will see in Chapter 6, the 'government approved' definition of best practice (namely the one built into the various pollution regulations) differs from that of the most rabid green activists in that the 'official' one has 'not entailing excessive cost' suffixed to it. For each of the various possible alternatives to each of the various activities studied in the audit, a variety of data, such as cost, availability, sourcing and installation parameters need to be obtained.

Workplan and responsibilities

It will be clear by now that undertaking an environmental audit – if it is to be done properly – is not something that should be done in an unstructured way. The framework of a basic workplan gives the team a series of task sequences to follow, and provides an assurance that critical activities are not inadvertently overlooked, or effort needlessly duplicated.

The outline project plan prepared in the previous planning stage of the audit will provide the basis for this, but having now undertaken the activities above, the team will have a better idea of the resources required, and what the likely timescales will be. In particular, decisions about timescales should be realistic ones – if something is going to take a longer time than originally envisaged it's usually better to plan that in at the beginning rather than run into flak for over-running later on.

A final point to make is that the timescale is not always of the business's choosing, and that sometimes it's the resources that have to be flexed, and not the timetable. As the environmental regulatory regime that businesses operate under becomes increasingly stringent, deadlines are being imposed from outside, such as standards needing to be met by particular dates.

Managements may take comfort, however, that in situations like this it is usually only *part* of the audit process that needs accelerating or the providing with additional resources. If a new regulatory requirement is known, then a business will either be able to quickly identify that its current standards are inadequate, and so go onto to the 'remedial' phase of option consideration and costing, or alternatively a quick examination will show that the standard is met and so no further action needs to be taken – at least for the moment.

Progress reviews and communication

A final part of the planning process is the building into it of suitable points to pause and review progess, both internally within the team itself, and also in conjunction with interested parties outside the team. These people primarily comprise two distinct groups – firstly, the team's 'sponsors', namely the senior management who set it up, and secondly, the representatives of those sections of the business that are being audited.

The name of the game, in both cases, is the avoidance of sudden and unpleasant surprises. Senior management will not appreciate either an audit that overruns, or for that matter one that suddenly delivers a weighty report pointing to massive environmental damage and the consequent need to spend millions on preventative measures. Quite apart from the financial and commercial aspects of this, no business's affairs are as secretly hidden away from public scrutiny as it would like, and minor bombshells of this nature have a habit of quickly finding themselves in the local press. Nor will matters be helped when it emerges that the review meetings with representatives of the local management of the area being audited have not taken place – especially when these would have shown that the findings were not as damming as described nor as expensive to put right as feared. For a variety of reasons, good communications are vital. The team needs to make sure that it's on the right track – and that those around it know where those tracks are leading. Anything else is just sloppy.

Getting started

We now have an area of the business to examine, a team to look at it, some indication of what we're aiming for – the outline policy definition – and a workplan. We've got a plan, we know who's doing what . . . so let's get started. First of all, we'll examine the opportunities for recycling.

4

Recycling and waste reduction

We now turn to recycling – and, even better than recycling, reducing the amount of waste in the first place. This chapter examines:

- **why business wastes so much**

- **how traditional accounting approaches encourage this – and what to do about it**

- **using less in the first place**

- **throwing away less**

- **recycling.**

Waste and the green business

The proportion of industry's manufacturing costs represented by expenditure on labour has been falling since the Industrial Revolution. The slice of the pie going on wages and salary costs has shrunk as more and more tasks become efficient and automated. In hi-tech industries such as electronics and computers, it's now down to around five per cent, or even lower.

What has this to do with recycling or waste reduction? Quite a lot – for the lower the proportion going on labour costs, the higher will be the proportion spent on materials. In the past, when labour costs were more important, industrialists boosted profits by tightly controlling labour costs. 'Time and motion' studies and the like served to stretch the efficacy of every penny spent on employing people. These days, shaving a few per-centage points off the wage bill can mean very little by way of a profit improvement – especially when compared to an equivalent percentage saving on the larger materials bill. Improved manufacturing yields – programmes to cut materials wastage, for example – are both green *and* profitable. A five or ten per cent reduction in material cost feeds straight through to the bottom line. So does a five or ten per cent cut in waste: the days of low cost (or even free) waste disposal are dying fast, as dumps fill up and legislators get more and more concerned about what goes into them: landfill dumping charges almost tripled in the years 1985 to 1992. And best of all, properly managed programmes to give materials a 'second life', through recycling, can make an even bigger impact to the environment and companies' profits.

The green business, as well as the profit conscious one, has three materials-related goals:

- use less

- throw away less

- recycle more.

These aren't new ideas – not even the recycling one. Waste recycling was one of the first readily identifiable green issues – the environmental group Friends of the Earth, for example, was pushing actively for greater use of recyclable and refillable packaging as far back as 1971. Indeed, large quantities of expensive raw materials, especially those where a ready market exists, have been recycled for years. The figures are quite impressive – in 1986, for example, over sixty per cent of steel production in the UK came from recycled materials. Recovery rates of other metals can be even higher: over ninety per cent from both industrial and post-consumer sources. For even where the raw materials themselves are cheap, it can make sense to recycle if the cost of the energy needed to convert them into usable product is high. This is largely the basis of the logic behind glass recycling, for example. The key raw material – sand – is cheap: the heat to turn it into glass isn't. Melting existing glass uses less energy than making it from scratch.

Yet straight away, as we saw in Chapter 2, we run into the fundamental difficulty that underlies most debates about the general principle of recycling. Ignore for the moment the actual recycling process: how is the physical material itself to be returned for subsequent reprocessing? Even where simple distinctions are possible, 'this is a glass bottle, this is an aluminium can, here are some old newspapers', domestic-based schemes still have a long way to go. Various alternatives are emerging, and the ultimate prognosis is generally favourable, but these are still only partial solutions. They chiefly work because they address the recycling of simply defined and homogenous materials: a bottle that is wholly glass, a newspaper that is solely paper, and cans that are readily identifiable as aluminium or steel.

65

But what about a failed lightbulb? What about an old television set? As assembled combinations of materials, they are difficult for consumers (or anyone else, with present technologies) to readily separate. Should they go into the bin for glass, plastic, or non-ferrous metal recycling? It's not at all clear cut. Domestic-based recycling typically suffers from this problem of diversity to a far greater extent than business-based recycling does. The crucial distinction between industry and home in terms of recycling is that the range of materials going into a business may be much smaller than that going into a household, and so is the range of materials going *out*. As we saw in Chapter 2, this gives businesses a number of opportunities. One is to trap and recycle materials themselves, internally, with their own processes and technologies. Another is to take advantage of the fact that their wastes, off-cuts and scrap are available in larger quantities and arrange for its recycling via a specialist operator. A domestic dustbin half full of mixed plastics is one thing; two tonnes of a plastic of a known composition quite another. A third option, as we saw in Chapter 2, is to try and extend the life of components and sub-assemblies by moving towards a greater use of 'exchange' or 'factory reconditioned' parts. The consumer, mechanic, electrician or other specialist, instead of simply throwing good components away through the failure or wear of a small part of it, installs a new one and return the old to the original manufacturer for reconditioning.

We will look at all these, and at the supposed cost penalties that are sometimes seen to surround them. Consider for a moment, though, the barriers to establishing this recycling culture and the resultant flow of materials. Materials where recycling is already well established – paper, glass, metals, etc – are those where there is both a cost incentive, certainly, but also – *and more importantly* – a ready market exists. Recycled glass, paper and metals find ready buyers – both buyers of the recyclable raw materials *and* buyers of the finished recycled product. In the case of the latter, they may be buying it simply because it *is* recycled, or because due to its recycled content it offers a price advantage. Those broad areas of opportunity listed above are chiefly *supply-based*: here is a potential material for recycling – what can we do with it, and how can we recycle it?

But it is important that businesses look at *demand-based* opportunities as well. By looking at itself and asking 'what recycled materials can we use?', the business performs a number of vital functions. Firstly, it uses other people's and other business's recyclable materials. A large generator of a particular waste or byproduct may not be able to either recycle it itself, or use recycled materials. Other businesses, however, could do so. Secondly, demand generates supply far more effectively than a supply can generate demand. Asking suppliers for recycled plastics, paper or whatever stimulates them in turn to ensure that they can supply what is being asked for. This ripples back up the supply chain, ultimately resulting in the businesses that create the particular wastes then being able to tap into a ready market for it. Result: a greener planet, less waste – and lower waste disposal costs – together with a more cost-effective business. A policy of buying recycled materials is every bit as green as recycling them in the first place. One is no use without the other – if no one uses the recycled waste, then there's no point in bothering to recycle it in the first place.

Nor may recycling continue in the future – in some aspects, at least – to be purely an optional issue. Packaging, of one sort or another, forms a high proportion of industry's total material costs. A rough rule of thumb is that the closer a business's products are to actual individual consumers (as opposed to other businesses or supply chain intermediaries) then the higher that proportion will be. At the moment, in the UK and in most of the EC, packaging's impact on the environment is largely unregulated. Traditional cost-inspired packaging forms apart – returnable beer and milk bottles, for example – there is little legal or commercial control of what happens to it after use. Most of it winds up simply wasted as rubbish of one sort or another, and burnt or dumped in a landfill. The tough green German laws on packaging recycling may well at some point be extended throughout the EC. It is still too early to assess the full impact of the law on German businesses: although transport packaging had to be recycled as from 1 December 1991, and secondary packaging from 1 April 1992, the full consequences of the law's final goal – total recycling of point of sale packaging – which came into force on 1 January 1993, are still working their way through the system. A wise business, however, would anticipate tighter strictures on packaging coming into force, and plan accordingly.

Looking at waste

So let's extend our basic environmental audit outwards to look in detail at some of the opportunities. To do this, we'll follow the audit through the logical sequence of first *reducing* waste, then *recycling* it. Our approach will be to repeatedly ask 'can we use less?', 'can we throw away less?', and 'can we recycle more of what we do throw away?'

USING LESS

1 Consider first reducing waste within your own organisation. Draw up a complete list, by type, of the:

(i)   process scrap and waste arising from the production process itself, if yours is a manufacturing business;

(ii) other 'repeat' waste emanating from the business's direct operations, such as rags, timber, packaging etc: manufacturing companies produce these, but so do shops and service operations;

(iii) office and people-related waste – paper, canteen wastes, drinks cans etc;

(iv) less regular 'one-off' wastes – old computers, typewriters and production machinery

that your organisation produces. Where does it come from? What has caused it to be thrown away? Could the quantities of process scrap and waste have been reduced through:

■ tighter purchasing specifications of raw materials?

- more exactly specified purchase quantities – for example lengths or widths that eliminate trimming waste and off-cuts?

- more tightly controlled production processes, so as to eliminate process variability?

- better defined (or better engineered) set-ups, so as to eliminate 'running in' waste?

- the elimination of unnecessarily tight quality and inspection standards?

- 'closed loop' systems to eliminate or reduce the evaporation of volatile liquids?

- in-plant recycling units to filter for subsequent re-use liquids such as oils, water and acids?

- redrafting specifications – especially those calling for the use of non-renewable resources?

69

Could the quantities of other waste be reduced by:

- using washable cleaning and protective materials rather than disposable ones?

- encouraging photocopying on both sides of sheets of paper?

- re-using 'scrap' paper as jotters, notepads etc?

- using electronic mailing ('email') for inter-employee correspondence?

- people using their own coffee mugs etc instead of dispensed paper or plastic cups?

THROWING AWAY LESS

2 What can be done to eliminate waste once products have been sold to consumers – that is, waste *outside* your immediate organisation, yet preventable (or at least minimisable) by actions taken *inside* it? Consider the following possibilities:

■ Designing products to use less raw materials – especially those using materials made from non-renewable resources. Drinks cans, for example, now have much thinner walls than they used to. An average drinks can in 1970 weighed 57g; twenty years on, it weighed 35g – a reduction of almost forty per cent. Lighter products, once the newly refined technology is mastered, are cheaper to both manufacture and transport, too. Modern washing machines use less water, detergent and energy than older models.

■ Procedures to sell substandard goods as 'seconds' rather than scrapping them: de-labelled rejects are commonly sold this way in the pottery, clothing and food industries.

■ Assisting consumers and recyclers by making products easier to recycle: marking on them the type of plastic that they are made from, adding a 'recyclable' reminder, reducing the number of different materials employed in them, and making such materials easier to detach or disassemble. Products comprising mixed materials, or unknown materials (or both) are less likely to be recycled. Early German experience, following the introduction of its packaging waste laws, is particularly instructive here:

Substitute for compound materials	
Elimination	40%
Polyethylene	20%
Polypropolene	12%
Waste Paper	4%
Paper/Cardboard	24%

■ Minimising packaging – most of which, almost by definition, is waste. Can packaging design be changed so as to incorporate fewer non-renewable materials? Can packaging design be changed so as to incorporate fewer different materials, in order to facilitate recycling? Can 'greener' materials be used – for example avoiding, or minimising the use of 'difficult-to-recycle' materials? Could bulk deliveries dispense with the need for packaging altogether? Failing that, can the amount of packaging provided be cut down? Again, early German experience on all these points is instructive:

Substitute for synthetic materials	
Elimination	38%
Polyethylene	13%
Polypropolene	3%
Waste Paper	5%
Recycled Materials	4%
Wood	2%
Paper/Cardboard	24%

71

■ Design products for an extended life. The age of the throwaway has largely gone – but do your products last as long as they could do? Commercial imperatives might seem to mitigate against this – the shorter the life, the more you sell – but this is illusory. Consumers are demanding longer lasting and more durable products anyway: they increasingly recognise the ecological unacceptability of the throwaway culture, as well as the higher costs associated with purchasing unnecessary replacements. As with many green issues in business, it's not only perfectly possible to transform your marketing message to exploit this, but highly desirable: products ranging from Volvo and Mercedes cars to Duracell batteries sell well on very explicit messages about outlasting their competition. And so do products, like kitchen appliances, designed to operate for the same performance, with less energy, water or other inputs – and to produce less waste at the same time.

■ Many products break down because consumer-replacable components or assemblies fail. In such a position, consumers often replace the whole product, because of difficulties in getting the spare part, or in getting the part at a fair price, or in getting just the part they need rather than a whole expensive sub-assembly. Review your aftersales service. Is it:

(i)   easy for customers to get the part they need?

(ii) economically effective?

(iii) easy for customers to get simple over-the-telephone repair advice?

(iv) straightforward for them to buy the parts that they need – in the absence of a service network, for example, can the customer telephone you and simply quote a credit card number? Complicated transactions put people off.

Again, the trick is not just to view actions taken on the above as extra costs and a burden, but as also possessing a marketing edge which you should exploit. The press love printing stories about eighteen-year-old washing machines kept going by a simple 25p valve or somesuch. These are worth thousands of pounds in free advertising – is your company getting its share?

■ Businesses throw away equipment and machinery – old computers, typewriters, photocopiers, industrial machinery and so on. This is pure waste. Consider some of the options:

(i)   Can the equipment be upgraded, rather than replaced? Would the addition of new electronic controls, replacement processors or whatever provide the same performance? Manufacturers might well prefer to sell you a whole new replacement – but are there procedures in place within your organisation to check first that upgrading is definitely *not* an option?

(ii) In the case of complex – or expensive – industrial equipment, is rebuild an option? Again, it is not as simple as buying in whole new pieces of plant, but in many instances is perfectly possible. If a piece of plant is still based on up-to-date technology, rebuild could offer a green alternative – and may result in not only a cheaper piece of equipment, but one with the option of customising and tailoring it to your exact needs.

(iii) Another option in the case of industrial equipment, space permitting, is to retain it. Businesses quite often find that commercial pressures force them to replace equipment well before the end of its productive life – with or without an upgrade or rebuild. A new piece of equipment is needed to match the speed or product characteristics that competitors are achieving. The question is: can the existing machine be kept and used in a dedicated fashion for production of other lines, thereby avoiding set-ups?

73

Careful calculations may needed – particularly in businesses where accountants run riot. Certainly, the old machine will be, perhaps, 'slower'. This *does not* mean, though, that continuing to produce on it means that you are necessarily in some sense 'losing money'. For a start, less time will be lost on the new machine for set-ups – yielding more capacity, and lower payments to operators for setting up. And if the old machine is truly dedicated, then no time at all will be lost on it for set-ups – and nor will it incur any running-in waste: it will always be set-up, ready to go at the push of a button. It's also worth bearing in mind that it will also be more fully depreciated than its replacement. The sums are worth doing: the outcome is not only a greener environment, but – with any luck – a more efficient business.

RECYCLING MORE

Having done all this, there will still be *some* waste that cannot be avoided. Some will be inside your own organisation, some will be at your customers – arising from the products that you have supplied them with – and some will have arisen from other people's quite separate activities – but which gives you an opportunity to recycle it if they cannot.

So let's continue the audit, turning now to ways of recycling this waste.

3 How can your products themselves incorporate a greater content of recyclable (*and* recycled!) materials? What scope is there for:

■ Recyclable spare parts and consumables? What happens to the old parts or products: could they – or the containers that they go in – be worth recycling? Can the motor industry's exchange system, where the return of spare parts capable of being reconditioned is encouraged by a pricing policy, be introduced in your business?

■ If you supply consumables, can you introduce refillable or returnable containers or dispensers, as with laser printer toner cartridges, for example? If your product comprises relatively small quantities of liquids or powders, could you introduce a 'parallel line' of slightly cheaper refill packs – a customer's first purchase being of the branded dispenser, subsequent purchases being less elaborate purchased refills?

■ A simplified mix of different plastics or metals in your products, so as to make them easier to recycle?

■ Products or components to be marked so as to indicate their composition, thus facilitating recycling?

■ Materials sourcing policies to be changed, so as to incorporate in your products a higher proportion of (readily available) recycled metals, plastics, glass and papers?

74

4 Packaging is a major source of waste. It is bulky, often designed for 'one-time use', and usually has a life span far shorter than the products that it protects. So: how can more of the packaging materials used in your business be recycled?

■ What opportunities exist for you to instigate a returnable packaging system with your customers? This is especially practicable in the case of businesses supplying other businesses, rather than consumers. Specialised 'long-life' plastic trays or pallets can be cheaper than 'one-time use' cardboard boxes, protect products better, and cut down on unpacking and waste costs at your customers. Already widely used in the motor industry, there is plenty of scope for extending the concept. The more regular a business's customers are, and the more it is in control of its own transport, the greater the potential for implementing returnable, multi-trip packaging.

■ Failing the above – perhaps because your business supplies consumers, or has a large number of small business customers – can you make your packaging from recycled materials? Can packaging – or at least some of it – be made from materials coming from renewable or recyclable resources?

■ Extending the two points above, to what extent can you require *your* suppliers to deliver their materials to you in returnable packaging? Or at least in packaging made from recycled materials?

■ Every day, a large quantity of packaging materials enter your business, probably passing through its goods inwards point – cardboard boxes, pallets, polythene wrapping etc. What happens to it? How much can be collected and saved for recycling – either directly, via being used to package your own outgoing products, or indirectly, via waste merchants?

5 A business's normal administrative operations also give rise to opportunities for recycling. In the case of shops and offices, these sometimes provide the only real scope. The focus here is on

75

recycling as much material as possible from one's own operations, and maximising the purchase of goods that are either wholly recycled, or have a recycled content. It's also about maximising the useful life of equipment, thus reducing the need to extract further quantities of non-renewable resources from the earth. Consider:

- Switching to recycled stationery. Photocopier paper, 'letterhead', envelopes and computer paper are all available in recycled form. Check to see that your business's photocopiers, printers and faxes can use recycled papers either as they stand, or with adjustment by your service engineer.

- Recycling your own paper waste. In reasonable quantities, this can be collected – and bought – by waste paper merchants. Sorting is sensible: prices are volatile, with the highest prices (and least fluctuation) being for clean 'white' business paper, including computer listing paper. If computer paper is available in quantity, it's worth separating this out on its own – it can be worth twenty times as much as general office waste paper. In general, papers with gums and resins (for example, books and envelopes), plasticised papers such as glossy brochures, cardboard, magazines and newspapers are rarely worth having a waste paper merchant collect. Delivering it yourself gets it recycled it *and* generates more cash. Talk to your waste paper merchants to establish the parameters: the quantities that they will collect, the prices they pay, and how they require the various grades of paper to be separated.

- Having canteen food wastes collected for direct re-use (pig or poultry food), or recycling – back to its original form, even, in the case of cooking oils – into animal feedstuffs.

- Providing bins by vending machines and canteen areas into which employees can place aluminium foil containers and drinks cans.

- Specify the use of reclaimed materials in any building work that is being undertaken.

An important point to bear in mind with some of the above opportunities is the problem of quantities. While companies may well be in a position to recycle food scraps, oils, paper and so on, the quantities involved may be so small that collection by an appropriate recycling contractor is uneconomic, or self delivery non-green because of the transport involved. There are two possible solutions.

The first is compacting. Many businesses are discovering that compactors are useful for squashing down their dry rubbish to minimise waste collection costs, which are essentially volume related. They also have a role to play in recycling. Compact, tidy cubes of waste fill storage space far more effectively, and also simplify handling. They may well be the answer – look in your Yellow Pages for suppliers.

The second solution involves 'bulking up' with other local companies, each of which may also have the same problem with small quantities of potentially recyclable material. One company on an industrial or trading estate can act as the repository for paper, another for scrap metal, another for plastics, and so on. The cash received from the recyclers can be split amongst the companies involved, or retained by the repository company, as agreed between the parties. They will probably need to come to their own inter-firm agreements about storage containers, paper compacting etc, but such arrangements often offer the best route forward for companies who would otherwise throw materials away because of the relatively slow rate at which they generate them.

Counting the cost

So what does all this cost – a lot, or a little? *Is* 'going green' prohibitively expensive? There are several answers – all of them really coming to the same conclusion: in many cases, not as much as might be expected – if at all. The arguments and costings will of course differ according to the circumstances of particular businesses. Some will naturally find individual audit areas more appropriate than others, but every business should find a number of opportunities listed above that are essentially *cost free*. Nor is it necessary to change the rules or fiddle the figures to show this. There are discussions in the media about 'green accounting' or environmentally-aware balance sheets and profit and loss accounts. These are attempts to provide a compensatory mechanism within a firm's accounts to show the environmental impact: a cut tree or used non-renewable resource is essentially treated as a 'free good' within conventional accounting practice: only the costs of logging, extraction and transport are formally accounted for. The environmental impact – a non-renewable resource has been lost forever, or a portion of the planet's biosphere has gone – appears nowhere. Green accounting tries to do this.

78

But it's not really necessary to get into environmentally-aware accounting to answer many of the questions to do with cost. So let's simply review the audit issues raised above with an eye on their cost implications in perfectly conventional corporate accounting terms.

As many of the 'so how much does it all cost?' issues are the same whichever area of business and the environment is being looked at – recycling, energy, the biosphere – this section is a very general one. Although it focuses on the recycling and waste reduction audit areas listed above, the basic principles that it espouses are those that need to be considered by businesses contemplating 'going green' in whatever respect. It therefore applies not just to this chapter, but Chapters 5, 6 and 7 as well.

TIME, LABOUR AND MATERIALS

Is it really costly, for example, to conduct an examination of ways of eliminating waste? (Or energy use, or whatever . . .) It takes time, certainly, and that time has to be paid for. But the time consumed (unless outside consultants are brought in) is generally an overhead anyway. People would still be paid for doing their normal jobs: the additional net cost of carrying out an audit is therefore very low – perhaps some specialist advice, monitoring equipment or publications.

Nor is the cost open ended. The audit will naturally tend to be less fruitful the longer the search goes on: one starts to run into the law of diminishing marginal returns. The first fifty ideas will probably be more significant than the second fifty, and so on. Assume a business says it will go on searching for green material savings until the costs of the search are outweighed by the incremental savings. That's environmentally friendly, and also sensible from the business point of view.

79

Once found, will audit items be expensive to implement? Some, possibly – others, certainly not. Again the diminishing returns concept is applicable: some ideas will generate bigger savings than others, and some ideas will be more expensive. There's management time of course, and again the overhead argument applies: it's being paid for anyway. There will also perhaps be, in many of them, a direct labour-related cost – in some cases, this will be the only additional cost area. More precise machine set-ups, more carefully defined production procedures, exactly specified material widths and lengths that demand more care in cutting or slitting: these are not the stuff of massive capital investment programmes or onerous and time-consuming managerial controls. They are simply good practice, albeit requiring a more careful approach to material conservation – and with a benefit that goes straight through to a company's financial bottom line, as well as contributing to a greener environment. So why are they not in place already? Why is it necessary to 'get them right' now, and why are they not already right? Are we sure that there is really any scope for improvement? Are there really any savings to be had?

The answers were touched upon right at the start of this chapter. Historically, managerial norms and standards have been focused very largely on labour efficiency: labour costs were high compared to others. If a little waste was incurred in the interests of lower labour costs, so be it. Let's not slow the job down to save a few pence: build in enough of a material loss rate in order to keep the job going at top speed. Fine, when many industrial tasks were largely manual, but the last twenty-five years have seen that logic sharply eroded. Computerisation, sophisticated electronic controls, faster and better industrial machinery – labour costs as a proportion of the whole are now a far smaller item, and material costs a far larger item, both in terms of material used and material having to be properly disposed of. (Not to mention energy costs – the subject of the next chapter.)

Yet these mentally built-in views of acceptable loss rates or yields often remain, long after technology has wiped out their reason for being. The result of this is that in many companies, the implied (and often only intuitively arrived at) ratio of the labour time that it's worth expending to achieve a saving in material is out of kilter. Thanks to increased automation and the like, the benefits of time spent now on improvements in material efficiency will continue to clock up. Many managers, when expressing doubt about the economic viability of some of this chapter's suggestions for waste reduction, simply haven't thought the issues through thoroughly enough within the context of their own companies. Do the sums – and surprise yourself . . .

INVESTING IN THE ENVIRONMENT

Some of the audit areas above are arguably only incidentally green anyway. Whilst manufacturers of drinks were no doubt happy to acknowledge the environmentally friendly result of making their can walls forty per cent thinner, one doubts that this was their primary goal. A straightforward improved material efficiency – particularly in an expensive metal like aluminium – is clearly worthwhile. Less weight means lower transport costs, too. Green, yes – but also a very attractive proposition in its own right.

Not all raw materials are as expensive as aluminium, but exactly the same principles still apply. Using less raw material in a product is both green *and* results in a direct cost saving in the product and indirect cost savings elsewhere in the supply and logistics chain – lower transport costs, lower internal materials handling costs and so on. Only at the margin, perhaps – but so were tiny direct labour savings, and businesses have always tended to regard those as worthwhile. The green business actively pursues such savings.

But sometimes – not surprisingly – it finds that although going green will reduce direct costs it requires an initial investment. It might be possible to redesign a product to use fewer raw material inputs, for example, but processing costs rise, or tighter tolerance equipment is required. Equally, a closed-loop system to minimise evaporation of volatile liquids will reduce waste, but only after an initial outlay. In the office and corporate business environment, an email system is a good example of where going green calls for more than just cutting out waste: an upfront investment is required in the hardware, software and training that is required.

So does the green business simply close its eyes and put its hands in its pockets? No – it is a green *business*, not a green charity. The first thing to do is assess opportunities for both their business and environmental impact. The transition to a green business will certainly soak up a lot of another scarce resource – management time. And there are plenty of potential projects for that time to be expended on – so how big an impact will any particular idea have? Don't waste time on minutiae: go for those that have a big impact on costs, or a big impact on the environment – or both.

The second stage is to assess the likely cost savings. Sometimes these are obvious – and sometimes they appear to be zero, or even negative. Do not be alarmed. Bear in mind that most business's accounting systems focus firstly on direct labour costs – as we have seen earlier – and secondly on cash. This is gradually changing, as businesses recognise the blindness that this leads to. A detailed discussion of subjects such as Activity Based Costing (which bases cost 'roll up' on *activities* like products' respective materials handling content) is outside the remit of this book, but cost savings might not be as slender as they can be at first perceived. One just has to look harder for them – and bear in mind the fact that your company's accounting systems are not geared up to provide the detail that you are looking for.

For example, a business might have a cost structure something like:

Direct labour	10%
Materials	30%
Overhead	60%

Looks familiar? Yet, as we saw above, many cost and management reporting systems focus a disproportionate level of attention on the direct labour element. Although potential savings in terms of direct materials are usually not too difficult to determine, savings through going green can also impact on the overhead side of the business, where many businesses have a relative blind spot. Deeper digging is often needed here, as businesses often lump lots of overhead costs together – and, even worse, sometimes regard them as a less exciting form of saving than a reduction in people, despite the relatively small part people play in the total cost structure. Saving five per cent of sixty per cent of the costs is far more rewarding than saving five per cent of ten per cent of them.

Sometimes the sums are fairly easy. An email system, for example, or washable cups instead of plastic ones – even after taking account of an estimate of an extra energy used. Sometimes they are more difficult to establish. The savings achieved by switching to a returns systems for used components or recyclable packaging are good examples of this. While the direct savings are straightforward to estimate, there are substantial direct costs to plug in, too – which are less easy to establish. In contrast to more conventional investments in machinery and equipment, investing in a recycling scheme involves uncertain costs as well as uncertain savings.

Both are volume related – and the initial set-up cost can indeed be substantial. By contrast, continuing to buy in new materials, perhaps emanating from the other side of the world, at first obviously looks easier and cheaper. The administration and management costs are all someone else's. Nevertheless, they *are* there, in the price that is paid for the new materials.

But there are compensatory savings, too. Fewer new materials to purchase, inspect, store and insure. Fewer cash outgoings, and possibly a lower working capital requirement. This book is not about going green at any cost: it is about being environmentally responsible enough to honestly work out the full costs and take decisions accordingly. Some costs can only ever be established by experiment: so set up a trial recycling scheme to firm them up rather than walking away because of the uncertainty.

If the green manager wishes to invest in something that has a low (or zero) rate of return, then fine. But this book is not asking him or her to do that: simply to comply with environmental legislation, and to do all they can within their existing capital investing criteria. Bear in mind, though, that what may work out as uneconomic today may not do so tomorrow: the costs of *not* going green are continuing to rise, and the demands of legislators and regulatory bodies are becoming more stringent. Tomorrow's sums may yield a different answer.

And on that note, let's now turn to consider an area of business's impact on the environment that provides one of the most extreme examples of this changeability: energy use.

5

Energy efficiency

This chapter covers green energy use within the business. We look at:

■ **how energy has historically been used – and wasted – and the impact on the earth's non-renewable resources**

■ **energy use and its side effects – acid rain, the greenhouse effect and the nuclear industry. Some forms of energy are greener than others – but is coal-generated electricity greener than that coming from nuclear power?**

■ **three energy strategies for businesses to follow**

■ **a green energy use audit checklist.**

Bags of energy

The last twenty years have seen two big shifts in the way that energy, as a green issue, is viewed. To start with, prior to the early 1970s, it was scarcely considered at all. Energy was cheap and plentiful, its use – at least in the developing world – growing rapidly, and often for purposes that could only bewilder our ancestors. Centuries of evolving civilisation had been principally powered through renewable energy sources. Wood was used for heating, tallow for light and animals for both transportation and motive power, such as grinding corn. Industrialisation started along the same lines, with water and wind powered mill wheels and wind powered sailing vessels.

Nor is this simply ancient history. Any traveller to the less developed parts of the today's world soon sees cultures operating at far lower levels of energy use – and also, like our ancestors, with a higher proportion of energy from renewable sources. While this is certainly something that many people are aware of in a vague sort of way, the actual figures behind it are quite startling. For instance, energy use in the countries of South Asia – principally India, Sri Lanka, and Pakistan – is twenty gigajoules per person a year. Energy use in Western Europe is a massive six times this, at 120 gigajoules per person per year. Consumers in North America and Australia are even more profligate, using on average 200 gigajoules per person per year – twenty times as much.

Continental averages like this hide huge discrepancies. The USA, for example, with just six per cent of the world's population, consumes thirty per cent of its energy. India, by contrast, has twenty per cent of the world's population, but consumes only two per cent of its energy.

The varying sources of that energy are also revealing. North America, along with Japan – the world's most intensive consumer of energy, generates less than three per cent of its energy from renewable sources, about two-thirds of which comes from hydro-power. In contrast, the poorest countries of South Asia – among the world's lowest overall consumers of energy – obtain well over half of their requirements from renewable energy – over eighty per cent of which is 'biomass' such as wood and dried cow dung.

Such figures, though, ignore a large source of renewable energy: food. In less developed countries, people wash their clothes and dishes by hand, and bicycle or walk to work. When there, if wanting to talk to someone a floor or so away, they'll go and see them instead of telephoning – walking up and down stairs to do so instead of using the lift. The 'fuel' for all this human activity is the daily food intake – all of which, by definition, is a renewable energy source. (Renewable, at least, if one ignores for the moment any questionable agricultural or fishery practices in producing it.)

By contrast, the way that western-style cultures seemed to be evolving in the post-Second World War period was the very antithesis of this. Instead of wearing warm clothes in winter and cool ones in summer, people tended to wear much the same things (particularly in formal or work environments) and relied on central heating and air-conditioning to compensate. Forget walking or cycling to work: vast urban conglomerations apart, more and more people eschewed public transport and drove themselves there instead. Automation and labour saving devices were seen as the keys to a better standard of living. The one car family was superseded by the two car family, machines were purchased to wash dishes and clothes, and traditional tools and devices were replaced by powered equivalents – electric drills, saws and lawnmowers in the home; electric typewriters, word processors and so on in the office.

87

The 1970s brought two shocks, hard on the heels of each other, to this view of energy as a cheap and plentiful commodity. The first was *The Limits to Growth*, by Donnella and Dennis Meadows et al, published in 1972, which pointed out not only how finite the earth's stocks of key resources such as fossil fuels actually were, but how soon they could be expected to run out. The timescales were frightening (although the authors' calculations have subsequently been revised), and people began to seriously contemplate the post-oil future.

The debate was still raging when, in conjunction with a boycott on oil exports to the US and the Rotterdam spot market, the oil producers' cartel OPEC quadrupled prices overnight in 1973.

For the first time since the Second World War, the Western world's consumers found out that they couldn't buy unlimited supplies of cheap energy – fuel so cheap, in fact, that much was wasted either by consumers or by producers. The first two distinguishable man-made objects reported by returning moon missions were the Great Wall of China and the giant flames from oil field gas flares in the Middle East.

The repercussions started resounding immediately as countries struggled to adjust. Fuel rationing schemes were brought in (although not in the UK – just), business struggled to cope with energy bills that seemed to have suddenly reached unthinkable levels, and governments urged energy conservation with mottos such as 'Save It'. For many consumers – particularly American ones, where gasoline prices at the time were only pence in terms of today's money – it was the first time that such a thought had really crossed their minds. Governments, too, had had little exposure to the concept. In the UK, one hapless government minister, when pressed for advice, was reduced to urging people to brush their teeth in the dark.

Experience came fast. With the February 1974 UK miners' strike – opportunistically timed less than six months after the oil shock – came lengthy power cuts for domestic users, a three day week for industry, and – ultimately – the downfall of Edward Heath's Conservative government. Energy conservation suddenly entered business's agenda – not necessarily (and in fact rarely) out of environmental concerns, but out of a wish to cut costs. Big industrial users apart, business's energy costs had previously been virtually fundable out of the petty cash. Suddenly, they became a far more significant part of the cost structure. Managers everywhere had an incentive to start down the road of energy conservation. Not only was there a short-term financial benefit – it saved them money – but there was a long-term environmental benefit, too: it extended the life of the planet's fuel reserves. But no sooner had business started to accept the need to be green when the timescales suddenly altered.

Energy use and the greenhouse effect

Whilst what we call the greenhouse effect had been theorised about by various scientists as far back as the late 1800s, it wasn't until the mid-1980s that the balance of scientific opinion elevated it from a theoretical possibility to a very real certainty. With this change in status came a change in the emphasis on the role of energy use within the environment.

As we saw in Chapter 1, the greenhouse effect is caused by various gases in the air changing the proportions of heat from the sun reflected back into space and held against the surface of the earth by the atmosphere's insulating blanket. Amongst these various 'greenhouse gases', the largest impact by far comes from carbon dioxide. Naturally occurring – each of us breathes it out as our own 'waste' as we turn oxygen and food into body energy – carbon dioxide is recycled by the Earth's 'lungs', its plant life, through the action of light energy and water in photosynthesis. Some, the 'oxide' part, returns to the air as oxygen. The 'carbon' part remains locked in the fibre of the plant – the so-called carbon reservoir. When burnt, either immediately as wood or dried cow dung, or perhaps millennia later as coal or another fossil fuel, the carbon recombines with oxygen to form carbon dioxide again.

But although the cycle is natural, its operation at the present time, thanks to mankind's activities, is not. Firstly, as we saw in Chapter 1, the capacity of the earth's lungs is decreasing. Every square mile of vegetation that disappears is a little less plant life to absorb carbon dioxide. Secondly, carbon that has accumulated in fossil fuel over hundreds of millions of years is now being suddenly released – analyses show that the levels of atmospheric carbon dioxide have increased by twenty-five per cent since 1800, and are currently rising at a half of one per-centage point a year. Most of this increase has occurred in the last quarter century. To put that half a percentage point in perspective, this means an increase of a further five percentage points in a mere decade – in other words, a fifth of the total increase from 1800 to the present!

Every time we consume energy from a carbon-based or fossil fuel, we add to the increase. Heating, lighting, motive power for machinery – they all consume fossil-fuel based energy. A therm of gas produces 5.3 kg of carbon dioxide, a litre of heating oil 2.6 kg and a kilowatt hour of electricity 1 kg – from the fossil fuels burnt to generate it. How many of each does your business consume in a year – and how much carbon dioxide does it contribute to the greenhouse effect as a result? Travel impacts, too. Every gallon of petrol, for example, produces 11.4 kg of carbon dioxide when burnt. Over a year, for a driver doing 20,000 miles in a car averaging 35 mph, that's 6.6 tonnes – around seven times the weight of the car itself. Each person stepping off a 4000 mile transatlantic flight has added a whole tonne of carbon dioxide to the atmosphere by doing so – a figure pro-rata for shorter trips within Europe, or longer flights to Japan or Australasia.

As companies and their managers wake up to the consequences of their energy consumption habits, the issue of fuel efficiency and energy conservation has entered the business agenda again. Conserving stocks for future generations was one thing – a changing climate today quite another.

90

Energy use, pollution and waste

It's not just carbon dioxide from fossil fuels that is a problem. There is the whole question of pollution, and of solid wastes created by our consumption of energy. Cars and trucks, boilers and power stations all throw out atmospheric pollution in the form of sulphur dioxide, various oxides of nitrogen, particulates, heavy metals, and other pollutants. Large coal-fired power stations can produce a tonne of sulphur dioxide every five minutes, and they are a prime source of the 130 million tonnes that mankind pumps into the atmosphere each year. Vehicles also produce sulphur dioxide, and in turn are a prime source of nitrogen oxide emissions.

Sulphur dioxide and nitrogen oxides are the main pollutants that cause acid rain – responsible for enormous devastation. UK emissions don't just harm our own environment – the prevailing winds over the UK also dump our emissions over other countries in Europe. Damage from acid rain is displayed by half of Germany's forests, and similar levels of damage are found in Switzerland and parts of Sweden. Over 2000 of Sweden's 14,000 lakes have been seriously acidified, and in 9000 of them fish stocks have suffered acidification damage. In Norway, 70 per cent of the lakes surveyed in the south of the country are acidified. Acid rain also causes massive damage in the US and Canada to forests, fish and lakes.

91

Various methods are available to reduce this pollution. In the UK, electricity companies are fitting flue-gas desulphurisation (FGD) equipment to some power stations to remove sulphur dioxide. FGD is already mandatory in Germany. Fitting catalytic converters to car exhausts helps reduce emissions of nitrogen oxides.

Nuclear power too, has its problems. As disasters at Chernobyl, Three Mile Island and Windscale demonstrate, things can and do go wrong – safety cannot be guaranteed. There are immense problems with disposal of spent nuclear fuels, reprocessing and long-term storage and security. Already the Irish Sea is one of the most polluted by radioactive waste in the world. And beyond this, privatisation of the UK electricity industry revealed that nuclear power is uneconomic against all other forms of energy supply. Indeed the economics is such that one pound spent on energy efficiency will save seven times as much energy as would be generated by investing one pound in nuclear power.

With today's clearer recognition of long-term energy efficiency, businesses have three alternative and complementary energy strategies to pursue instead, and which *are* genuinely green. These are:

- Reducing the 'base load' consumption of energy, both by using less energy in the first place, and by using what energy *is* consumed more efficiently. This, for the average business, is by far the most significant of the three strategies.

- Recycling waste energy. As with the recycling of physical materials and products, energy can sometimes often be usefully recycled, too. Whilst this is of more practical significance to larger companies and industrial energy users, there are still points of note for even the smallest business.

- Using greener primary sources of energy. At the level of individual businesses, this is a less significant strategy. Apart from the truly vast enterprises – oil companies and the like – most businesses have to take the energy sources that are made available to them, certainly in terms of their bulk requirement. But, as we will see, there are still some opportunities to substitute renewable sources of energy for non-renewable ones, and to use energy forms that emit less carbon dioxide.

So how should these three strategies for green energy use be applied in *your* business? Let's take a look at each of them, and establish what scope exists.

Reducing base load consumption

There are lots of ways to cut a business's base load consumption. Thanks to high energy prices, most of them are attractive options financially, too. As with conservation in the home, basic measures are not expensive and pay for themselves very quickly.

The parallel ends there. Contrary to what one might think, offices and factories are far less energy efficient than homes. (After all, most business premises are only occupied for ten or so of the twenty-four hours, and then usually during the day, when lighting and heating requirements are at their lowest – so they *ought* to be more efficient!) There are many reasons for this. Large expanses of single glazing, for example (not to mention all those office blocks with outer surfaces that seem to comprise nothing but glass), that call for extra heating in winter and air conditioning in summer. Corridors and offices with lighting diffusers that let through only twenty per cent of the illumination generated. Heating, lighting and air conditioning systems that operate on a 'floor at a time' or even 'building at a time' basis. Warehouses where the heating struggles to maintain an ambient (not to mention legal) winter temperature even though all the large doors through which the trucks drive are wide open. Waste – simply because preventing it seems to be on nobody's job description. And so on.

93

The following audit ideas are intended to act as a useful framework for starting to examine and reduce these areas of inefficiency and waste. Full audit details, as well as practical help, can be obtained both from the Department of Energy's Energy Efficiency Office (see Appendix 1 for address) and a business's own local supplier of gas and electricity.

ENERGY CONSUMPTION AND THE WORKING ENVIRONMENT

1 For what periods are buildings heated and lighted:

a) hours per day;

b) days per year? How do these relate to occupancy periods?

2 Is the building insulation as good as it might be? Check:

a) walls, floors and roofs;

b) hot water tanks and pipe runs;

c) doors and windows. What about draught excluders?

3 What is the temperature set to?

a) Could it be reduced (in winter) or increased (in summer)? Each 1°C reduction that the thermostat can be lowered from 22°C reduces energy usage by eight per cent.

b) Are individual radiators fitted with thermostats? What are these set to?

4 Is ventilation excessive or unnecessary? (This is often the major cause of heat loss.)

a) Are windows left permanently open or ajar?

b) Are windows used as a form of temperature control – instead of turning the thermostat down? (Do workers actually know where the thermostat or temperature control is located? Who has the authority to change the settings?)

c) Are doors left permanently open, or open for long periods?

d) Do loading bays etc have heavy gauge polythene heat retainers – and are these hanging down, and not tied back?

e) Does your air conditioning or refrigeration plant operate without any CFCs? Not strictly an energy consumption issue, but CFCs are powerful 'greenhouse gases' and commercial scale non-CFC alternatives are available and winning against other options (see Appendix 1 for details).

5 How efficient is the boiler?

a) Is it more than seven years old? (If so, it's probably worth replacing – newer models are far more efficient.)

b) Is it a gas- or oil-condensing type? (Gas condensing boilers are more than eighty-five per cent efficient, compared with sixty to seventy per cent for a normal gas boiler. Oil condensing boilers offer a saving of up to thirty per cent. They are more expensive (and difficult to get hold of) but offer good payback periods. See Appendix 1 for suppliers.

c) What is the actual boiler thermostat set to? Can it be reduced?

d) What sort of timer is fitted? Programmable electronic ones, as opposed to simple mechanical ones, can offer much more finely tuned control and energy savings.

e) Is the boiler serviced at frequent enough intervals? Can the heating engineer recommend the installation of additional fuel economy devices, such as a temperature cut-out to prevent 'short cycling'?

6 How efficient is the lighting?

a) How brightly lit are the building interiors? Do people need it to be that bright? (Many offices have internal lighting levels far brighter than people have at home.)

b) Is light energy being lost in diffusers?

c) What use is made of natural light? Could more be made – siting peoples' desks and workspaces next to windows, for example?

d) Are low energy lightbulbs in use? These, although more expensive initially, are five times as efficient and last eight times as long. Replacing a conventional 100W bulb with a 20W low energy one can give a net saving of more than £32 over the bulb's lifetime.

e) If lights are in ceiling clusters (of say four), what is the effect on light levels through simply removing a bulb? Or two?

f) What are the procedures for switching lights off at the end of the normal working day? How much lighting is left on to cater for the illumination needs of just a handful of people working late?

g) Are unused areas or offices lit? (Semi-fixed office dividers can often split a group of lights controlled by a single switch into several offices or rooms – not all of which may be in use.)

h) Can external security lighting be adapted so that it is movement responsive, rather than being permanently on?

7 Would the use of low-tariff off-peak electric storage heating be viable? (This is not only cheaper, but tends to come from the electricity generators' lowest-cost and more efficient power stations.)

8 How efficient are appliances and office equipment?

a) Do photocopiers etc have both a stand-by mode and a copy mode? If so, is the stand-by mode actually being used by people?

b) Are suppliers asked to provide power ratings when appliances and equipment are purchased? What part do these play in the purchasing process?

c) Do electric hand driers have movement sensitive triggers, or simply timed push on-off buttons? Would towels suffice?

d) How much drinking water is heated at a time? Are kettles or water urns used? Are water urns left on at night and over the weekend?

e) Do some staff have their own coffee machines, fans, or fan heaters? Are these really necessary?

ENERGY CONSUMPTION AND INDUSTRIAL PROCESSES

This section, by necessity, is briefer than the preceding one. Just as industry varies enormously, so does the applicability of various energy efficiency techniques. The questions that are appropriate for a chemical plant are not the same ones that apply to a light engineering factory. Some points are also excluded because they repeat points made above – the possibility of using low-tariff off-peak power, for example, and many of the points relating to heating and insulation.

1 How efficiently is plant and machinery being operated? Can friction, loadings and waste be reduced?

a) Are there leaks of steam, hot water or compressed air?

b) Are pipes and tanks adequately lagged?

c) Is heat radiating from 'hot spots' on process plants such as stress relieving or annealing furnaces? Use infra-red thermography if necessary to detect it.

d) Is planned maintenance carried out – or carried out frequently enough? Even slight winding faults on electric motors sharply degrade their efficiency.

e) Are lubrication procedures adequate – both in terms of machinery and machining processes that require lubrication, for example cold reduction of metal? Unnecessary friction increases machine loadings and therefore power consumption.

f) Is machinery being left on unnecessarily – for example conveyor belts left rolling through lunch breaks?

g) Are processes running at the lowest possible temperatures? Do motors have much higher ratings than are needed?

h) Can single-speed pumps and fans be replaced by more responsive two speed ones – or even better, by fully responsive variable speed ones – to avoid unnecessary effort being expended?

i) In the same vein, are fans or pumps struggling against blockages or obstacles? Can pipe runs be re-engineered to eliminate 'hydraulic resistance'? (A 90° bend made by bending a piece of pipe rather than by using a plumbing fitting is far more efficient.)

2 Are individual handling activities reviewed from the point of their energy efficiency?

a) Can conveyor belts be replaced by free-running roller tracking?

b) Can machining sequences be laid out so as to make use of gravity – consistently rolling parts and components 'downhill' rather than up and then down, up and then down and so on?

c) Can activities be simply cut out? Do components need to have so many holes drilled in them – could four suffice instead of five, for instance?

d) Can activities be linked, so as to eliminate intra-operation storage and handling?

e) Is energy being 'invested' in a part, only to then be wasted, and so need re-inputting? (Could castings be placed in a pre-extrusion furnace whilst still hot from the casting process, for example, rather than being allowed to cool down first?)

f) Are there alternative processes that use less energy for the same result – eg specialist applications of electricity such as radio frequency heating, or small-scale gas-fired combined heat and power systems?

ENERGY CONSUMPTION AND TRANSPORTATION

There are significant opportunities to make the transportation of both people and materials far more energy efficient. This is a key way for businesses to reduce their base load energy consumption. Unlike the preceding checklists, though, many of these opportunities are far more ongoing and continuous. Insulating buildings and replacing boilers are essentially 'one off' activities. Transportation decisions are being made all the time.

And many of them are being made with insufficient regard to both their energy efficiency and their wider environmental implications. There are a number of reasons for this. As with many green issues, people's instinctive reactions are for trimming back their existing practices and arrangements rather than for undertaking entire wholesale rethinks of the process. Cultural imperatives are important in this: people still feel that serious business has to be carried out face to face, rather than (say) over the telephone. And when they travel, people will often want to use their own vehicles rather than going by public transport. People travel to work, rather than work travelling to people. Commercial practices as well as legal stipulations often involve the physical transportation of pieces of paper, rather than electronic codification or facsimile of it. There is, once one really starts looking, a lot to go at: an awful lot of our daily transport-related activities, practices and customs date from an era when fuel was cheap and no one had heard of the greenhouse effect. Consider the following in *your* business.

1 How much travel can be eliminated?

a) Can the numbers of people travelling to an event or meeting be cut down?

b) Could video-conferencing suffice, instead? The technology is still in its infancy, and expensive, but should be considered as an alternative to regular long distance travel.

c) If cars are used, can transport be pooled, with several people travelling in one car?

d) Is the journey really necessary – can phone calls or letters suffice instead? (Possibly slower, possibly less 'personal' – but offering big savings in unproductive time and travel budgets.)

e) Are people travelling to work unnecessarily? Could 'tele-commuting' be viable for certain members of staff?

f) Many journeys are short ones – and cold engines consume twice as much fuel as warm ones. Can people walk instead? And if your business is on a large site, could a system of pooled bicycles cut down the number of short car journeys?

g) Could the location for the meeting or event be changed so as to reduce the net amount of travel that the attendees need to make?

h) Are *goods* being moved unnecessarily? Japanese-style management approaches such as 'Just in Time' can substantially cut down the numbers of times goods need to be handled. Fork-lift trucks are vehicles, too!

2 Can necessary travel be made more energy efficient?

a) Can public transport be used? Buses and trains are up to five times as fuel efficient per passenger transported – as well as offering passengers opportunities to work en route. Although public transport may well be a 'slower' option in terms of total door-to-door time, it can consequently result in a significant increase in *productive* time.

b) Are people driving their cars and trucks in an economical and efficient manner? Bear in mind:

i) High speeds burn fuel inefficiently – driving at 70 mph consumes thirty per cent more fuel than driving at 50 mph.

101

ii) Maintain vehicles properly: correctly tuned engines, tires inflated to the right pressure and so on.

iii) Avoid carrying unnecessary weight.

iv) Sharp braking just throws energy away – thinking ahead can avoid it. Steady, consistent driving is far more fuel efficient than erratic bursts of speed followed by sharp braking.

c) Are fuel efficient vehicles being selected? The fuel efficiency of cars and trucks varies widely. Manufacturers are legally obliged to publish comparative statistics – are they an active part of your selection criteria? Set a goal of having each new vehicle being more fuel efficient than the one that it replaces.

d) Are the vehicles using more appropriate fuels being considered? Would gas or electric fork-lift trucks be better? In relation to the types of journey made by your vehicles, would petrol or diesel engines be best? (The Department of Transport publishes fuel consumption figures annually, based on standard tests.)

Recycling waste energy

Strictly speaking, energy is never 'consumed', even though we refer to it as being used or expended. It is, however, changed or transmuted: the latent energy in petrol is consumed to propel the car forwards. When we put on the brakes, that energy doesn't disappear – it is turned into heat, through friction generated as the braking action slows down the wheels. Machinery, processes and electrical appliances often give off heat as a result of either friction, electrical resistance or leakage. This is useful, because heating comprises a large part of total energy usage – up to ninety per cent in the typical domestic residence or office, for example. Think about the following:

1 In the office environment, what opportunities exist to make use of heat given off by electrical equipment such as computers (especially large ones) and photocopiers? 'Computer rooms' are especially attractive from this point of view: hot enclosed spaces – yet often with fans (or worse, air conditioners) to pump the heat out into the outside air. Why not divert it instead into the office atmosphere, or, via a simple heat exchanger, into preheating the air or water used by the heating boiler?

2 Can boiler or process condensates be recovered rather than wasted?

3 Can waste be used as a fuel? (Check the appropriate pollution legislation first – but given the appropriate furnace, the calorific value in non-reclaimable or recyclable materials can be retrieved.)

4 Can manufacturing processes be converted so as to use materials with a higher intrinsic energy content? Most recycled products, including paper, have higher intrinsic energy contents. Metals based on scrap, for example, reduce the overall need to use power to refine from virgin ore. In the case of aluminium, for example, this produces a large part of the ninety-five per cent cost reduction. And a policy of reclaiming, reconditioning and recycling components – as with exchange parts in the motor industry, for example – saves not just the material content, but also the energy needed to process that material. Every reclaimed casting is a another casting's worth of cold metal that does not need to be heated to melting point.

5 The vast majority of energy is for the generation of heat, either for space, water or process heating. No single piece of heat generating equipment is one hundred per cent efficient (and in fact most are in the thirty to forty per cent range: there are always leaks and heat exhausts. Given this happy coincidence (lots of waste heat, and plenty of demand for it), review every single significant item of heat generating equipment that the business has – starting with the top ten or top twenty, for instance. What happens to the heat that they waste or leak – and what *could* happen to it instead?

103

GREENER PRIMARY ENERGY SOURCES

We've looked at reducing the energy consumption base load by cutting out waste and improving efficiency. We've looked also at lowering the primary energy input by recycling 'waste' energy: we now have a core level of consumption. Is there scope for making it greener still? Yes – but not much.

The greenest possible energy comes from wholly renewable sources, and is non-carbon dioxide emitting. But although a nation can decide to make massive switches to tidal, wind or hydroelectric power, businesses can't. In practice, no business is able to change entirely to wholly green sources of energy. What they can do, however, is to substitute *parts* of their base load usage for green (or greener) alternatives. It may not be very much – but it's a start.

1 A very simple switch can be made when travelling. Taxis (of the London 'black cab' variety) often produce more carbon dioxide per passenger mile than other forms of transport. Use other public transport if possible.

2 In the UK, large consumers of electrical power now have the option of buying from power suppliers other than their local distributor, one of the former Electricity Boards. These in turn buy electricity from of one of the power generators, such as National Power or PowerGen. The relative 'greenness' of these sources differs – and is constantly changing. Electricity generated from coal is both dirtier (acid rain) and less efficient: less than a third of coal's thermal energy is transformed into electricity in one of the older style power stations; up to thirty-nine per cent in newer ones. Forty-five per cent of gas's thermal energy is converted – and results in less acid rain. Proportions coming from nuclear energy differ, as do proportions from hydroelectricity and other green (or greener) sources. By 1995, for example, National Power is aiming to convert 650,000 tonnes of domestic and commercial waste a year into electricity as an alternative to landfill dumping.

3 More radically, electricity users located by a stream or river may be able to utilise it to turn a generator – the old fashioned water wheel idea, but this time generating motive power. It won't make a big difference, but it will make some – and it does send a very positive signal to employees and other stakeholders about the business's green credentials. Apprentices or the local tech-

nical college may be happy to take the task on as a training project – ask around.

4 Farms and remote dwellings have used wind-powered generators to provide electricity or to pump water for many years. New designs are more efficient, but will obviously only generate part of a business's power requirements. Planning consent may well be required. See Appendix 1 for suppliers and contacts.

5 In the same vein, solar heating of 'domestic' hot water (that is, principally for washing) may be an option. Even in winter, the systems can produce a useful amount of pre-heating to reduce the energy input required to bring it to normal temperature. Depending on system size and usage, hot summer days could cut electrical or other heating of water to virtually zero. Solar heating is definitely a 'proven' technology in the UK, albeit one with a longer payback than at first envisaged – in part due to high expectations in their early days, but also due (ironically) to falling energy costs. The lower the price of non-renewable energy sources, the less attractive is the investment to switch to renewable ones – even if free. Practical considerations, such as the availability of a south-facing roof, are key.

6 Users located by streams or rivers can also heat water using the 'heat pump' principle. A temperature gradient of only a degree or so can still produce useful amounts of heat – and in fact, the efficiency of the device declines the higher the temperature over which it is required to pump. In practice, using a river as a source and producing heat at about 50°C gives a performance of about two – meaning that every one kilowatt of electricity used in pumping will produce two kilowatts of useful heat. Appendix 1 provides more details. As with (3) above, it may make a useful training project for apprentices or the local technical college – but talk to the National Rivers Authority first.

6

Preventing pollution

- **business, pollution and the law**
- **The Environmental Protection Act 1990**
- **what the Act covers**
- **licensing requirements and 'BATNEEC'**
- **an audit checklist.**

The long green arm of the law

In looking at recycling and energy in the previous chapters, we've concentrated on highlighting the latent potential for businesses to be green, and tried to show that an environmentally friendly approach to business need not conflict with managers' profitability and efficiency goals. Choosing the green route is not the path to penury that is sometimes painted. The thrust of this chapter is rather different. As far as pollution is concerned, going green is an obligation rather than an option.

'Obligation' in two senses, rather than one. Chapters 1 and 2 touched on some of the damage to the environment that business activities have caused over the years. Overenthusiastic (or ignorant) exploitation of the earth's resources is one thing – but wilful poisoning of the biosphere through thoughtlessness, lack of care and poor controls quite another. Sometimes this manifests itself through accidents such as Seveso or Chernobyl: 'one-off' incidents caused through failings in control or containment systems. Thankfully, environmental pollution on this scale, though tragic, is rare. More insidious, and unfortunately far more common, is the everyday pollution arising through inappropriate means of waste disposal.

Take the US Love Canal disaster, for example. In the 1930s, a chemical company near Niagara Falls in the state of New York dumped waste chemicals, stored in steel drums, into a muddy ditch. Twenty years later, the ditch was filled in, a school built on top, and a community called Love Canal created by speculative builders. Twenty years further on, the drums were leaking, the area was pervaded by a strong smell, and a slime emerged that burned holes in shoes. Medical symptoms included nervous disorders, liver problems and a high level of miscarriages. A Federal Emergency was declared, leading to evacuation and a major cleanup. Eighty-two different chemicals were identified, eleven of them suspected or known to cause cancer. The incident highlighted a whole series of failures, problems and potential pitfalls. Not surprisingly, similar incidents abound, and doubtless many more will come to light.

The damage has already been done: countless dumps, landfills and contaminated sites around the world contain chemical cocktails. One such, Stump Creek Gap – again in the state of New York – achieved brief notoriety when its 25,000 steel drums containing toxic waste were swept away by flood waters. And for a time, a trade flourished in shipping drums of waste to poor African and East European countries that lacked both the facilities to do anything with it, and the controls over its proper storage. Thankfully, an international convention in 1989 banned this. But a legacy of dumps, in the West as well as the developing world, remains. Some are known, but others are not; some still intact (in the sense of still being within containment vessels, at least), others leaking or simply buried in the ground or tipped into the sea.

Nor should groundwater and air pollution be overlooked: a smokestack belching toxic fumes, or a drain flowing with chemical runoff, can be just as injurious, if not more so. For although the concentration of toxicity is weaker, the area affected (and so the number of people exposed) is far greater. The effects of these two in particular in areas of Eastern Europe would take hundreds if not thousands of years to heal, even if output stopped tomorrow. Factories in the immediate vicinity of Katowice in Poland, for example, spew out from their factory chimneys seven tonnes of cadmium, 170 tonnes of lead and 470 tonnes of zinc dust every year. And it's not just Eastern Europe where there are damaging levels of metal pollution. In 1990, we put into our UK coastal waters as much as 3920 tonnes of zinc, 670 tonnes of lead and 63 tonnes of cadmium. Although concentrations of toxicity are naturally highest in the immediate vicinity, Chernobyl provided a rare real life experiment in illustrating quite how far toxic dust can travel.

109

Preventing further pollution on this sort of scale, from whatever source, is simply good sense: although especially noteworthy – or notorious – examples like Love Canal rightly shock, the cumulative effects of hundreds or thousands of smaller scale incidents amounts to much the same thing. We all are ultimately tainted by our own effluent one way or another, and owe it to ourselves – and our descendants – to leave the planet much as we found it.

But there is a stronger form of obligation. As we saw in Chapter 2, the early history of environmental protection – such as it was – was essentially one of legal measures against *active* environmental damage, that caused by pollution. Although recent years have seen the environmentally related body of law substantially broadened, they have also seen controls on pollution tightened still further. New laws, such as the 1990 Environmental Protection Act, are both more exacting than their predecessors and also wider in scope.

For example, *every* business, without fail, is potentially covered by it: any form of waste arising on commercial premises is a 'controlled waste' within the meaning of the Act. The Act is also tougher in its treatment of pollution from waste: it imposes a legal 'duty of care' on businesses and their corporate officers, backed by criminal sanctions, not to pollute. This too is far reaching, and takes the whole issue of environmental legislation into new areas. Environmental law was previously concerned with the perpetrators of pollution – those who carried out the actual illegal dumping of toxic waste, for example. But the Environmental Protection Act also places a legal liability upon the business whose waste it originally was. A company has a duty of care to do what is reasonable to see that its waste is safely and properly disposed of and to ensure that those who dispose of its waste are registered to do so: it cannot simply wash its hands of the problem by having a contractor come in and get rid of it.

110

The Act is set out in nine parts. Part I covers the imposition of 'integrated pollution control' – in theory a move away from the previous piecemeal approach – on major potential polluters, and the application of air pollution controls on those considered to be less serious risks to the environment. Part II of the Act relates to waste on land, with particular requirements in respect of the 'duty of care', waste management licenses and improper handling of waste. Part III covers statutory nuisance and clean air, whilst Part IV covers litter. Part V updates the provisions of the Radioactive Substances Act 1960, and Part VI imposes requirements on those handling genetically modified organisms.

Later Parts are even more obscure. Part VII handled the break up of the former Nature Conservancy Council into its English, Scottish and Welsh replacements, Part VIII covered a ragbag of miscellaneous provisions – pollution at sea, dog fouling and stubble burning, to name but three. The final Part, Part IX, covers the inter-relationship between the Act and other parallel community and international obligations.

In this chapter we will explore in detail how businesses can fulfil these twin obligations – the 'ethical' (but ultimately optional) obligation placed on them as global citizens, and their legal responsibility as it stands at present under UK and EC law. We are concerned here primarily with Part I of the Act, which is the aspect of it that impinges most widely on the business community, and the duty of care obligation contained within Part II. Sadly, as will become clear in the rest of this chapter, many businesses fail to meet either of these. A combination of ignorance and misunderstanding, coupled to the very real speed at which environmental standards have changed, means that existing custom and practice within many firms still falls far short of the ideal – or, for that matter, the lawful.

This chapter is essentially addressed to managers in a 'typical' business. It also focuses mainly on 'core' business activities. There is an interconnectedness with many green issues, and pollution is no exception. The parallel has been made between waste and recycling – the subject of Chapter 4 – and pollution. There are also very strong links between energy use and pollution. If one man's waste is another's pollution, then equally polluting are the exhaust fumes and carbon dioxide from his transport, and the greenhouse gases from his heating, lighting and power consumption. Rather than repeating any of what has just been said, we concentrate here on the pollution potential of core production processes and activities.

As we saw on page 32, there are a bewildering variety of environmental laws which have come into place over the years to control various forms of pollution from these. Again, we are not concerned in this book with the esoteric, but with the general. Managers engaged in such activities as running vast chemical plants, operating toxic waste incinerators or transporting radioactive substances by sea – to name but three – are generally aware of their responsibilities and are regularly monitored on their compliance with them. The potential hazards are far greater, and the consequent degree of scrutiny much higher.

Who, me?

In fact, Part I of the 1990 Environmental Protection Act (henceforth 'the Act') helps to make this distinction clear. It was the latest in a long line of environmental laws stretching back to early legislative controls such as the 1956 Clean Air Act. As we shall see, the Act broke new ground in several key areas. The first of these was to segregate businesses according to the environmental risk and hazard that they represent.

Essentially, it separates firms into three sorts: 'Part A' businesses, 'Part B' businesses – and those that are neither. Part 'A' businesses can be thought of as those more significant – or specialised – environmental risks. For these, the Act brought in the concept of Integrated Pollution Control, requiring that both the manufacturing process and the disposal route for wastes be chosen so that the releases have the least effect on the environment as a whole. The regulatory body for Part 'A' processes is Her Majesty's Inspectorate of Pollution (HMIP) which is required to consult with all other statutory consultees, such as the National River Authority, the Health and Safety Executive, Local Authorities and Statutory Nature Conservation bodies, on all Part 'A' process applications. (Except in Scotland, where it falls to Her Majesty's Industrial Pollution Inspectorate – HMIPI – and the seven river purification authorities.)

The requirements of Part 'A' businesses in respect to compliance with the Act are very specialised. In theory, anyway – in schoolmaster's terminology – 'they know who they are' (or at least *should* know who they are!), and this book can only go a small part of the way towards meeting their needs. Indeed, Part 'A' businesses have to appoint particular named officers who hold a responsibility for meeting the environmental provisions of the Act.

113

Essentially, these are to ensure that *all* emissions into the environment are in accordance with the appropriate standards. These standards are not specified in the Act itself, which is largely a piece of 'enabling' legislation. Nor are they wholly set down in the relevant regulations, guidance notes and so forth that are in force. In a radical departure, the Act introduced the concept of emission levels set by 'the best available techniques not entailing excessive costs' (BATNEEC). This is both a *moving* target – as technologies evolve and improve – and a potentially tougher one. Direct discharges to water from Part 'A' processes, for example, must still meet the standards required by the National Rivers Authority, *but must also meet still higher standards if the use of BATNEEC requires this.*

It is up to HMIP to decide, on an ongoing rolling basis, what exactly BATNEEC implies for a Part 'A' business. The Act also requires businesses to have in place both appropriate systems and control mechanisms to prevent excess levels of emissions, as well as detailed contingency plans for containing and controlling any that do occur. Without these being in place, and without them meeting the requirements of regular set inspections, no Part 'A' business is allowed to operate.

Not surprisingly, the Act goes into significant detail as to which processes or types of business fall into Part 'A' or 'B'. Part 'A' businesses are essentially those operating one or more of a number of carefully specified industrial processes – probably totalling around 5000 installations throughout the UK. They fall into two types. Firstly, businesses carrying out latently potentially environmentally damaging industrial processes – such as those involving asbestos, uranium, cement manufacture and oil or metal refining, in addition to a number of chemical processes. The risks here are obvious. The second category comprises businesses performing what are essentially 'less risky' Part 'B' operations, *but* on a scale large enough to warrant being regarded as appropriate for Part 'A' controls. A business with a brass furnace of less than five tonnes holding capacity is counted as being subject to Part 'B' controls, for example: above that limit and it joins the ranks of Part 'A'.

The responsibilities faced by operators of Part 'B' processes are less stringent. They too have to have their potentially polluting processes licensed and authorised under the Environmental Protection Act, but only in respect of emissions to the atmosphere. Waste-, water- and other appropriate regulations also apply from other legislation. In all, it is estimated that around 28,000 industrial installations are rated as falling under Part 'B' of the Act. The regulatory body in respect of a Part 'B' business is its local authority, which determines for each licensed business in its area the appropriate BATNEEC standard.

Business-related air pollution is an important source of atmospheric pollution: quite ordinary businesses that bear no rela-

114

tion to the sorts of chemical manufacturing processes which resulted in horror stories like Love Canal still produce atmospheric emissions. In the past, such businesses were less strictly controlled, as local authorities had to rely on statutory nuisance legislation, prosecuting polluting businesses under public nuisance laws. In practice, this meant that businesses not covered by HMIP and located away from complaining neighbours could effectively do what they liked.

The Act broke new ground in enforcement, too. Prosecutions for breach of operating conditions can be initiated not just by the enforcing authority but by a member of the public. Furthermore, Section 157 of the Act specifically enables the direct punishment of directors or managers if the offence was caused either with their consent or through their negligence.

115

Clearly, an important question for any business is which (if either) part of the Act it falls under. However, despite the publicity surrounding the Act coming onto the statute book, businesses have been slow to comply. Of the 5000 or so Part 'A' sites being phased in over a period of five years (full details are available from HMIP), for example, only 253 had filed the appropriate applications by May 1992 – over a year after the Act came into force on 1 April 1991. (In England and Wales, anyway – Scottish businesses were given a further year in which to comply.) Evidence to date in terms of Part 'B' sites seems similar: the industries affected are diverse and often small. They are falling under strict control for the first time, and their whereabouts is often unknown to many local authorities. Large numbers of managers simply do not realise that the controls apply to them. Indeed it seems that as of the summer of 1992, some twenty per cent of businesses operating Part 'B' processes had not even lodged applications for authorisations. Any business must therefore ask itself, before expending managerial effort on non-mandatory green projects, whether it is unwittingly failing to comply with those environmental obligations that carry legal weight.

Although it is reasonable to expect that operators of Part 'A' processes will tend to be brought into line before Part 'B' businesses, there is no cause for Part 'B' businesses to feel complacent. Compliance in both cases is a legal requirement, and local authoritiesare required to seek out non-complying businesses within their boundaries.

The following summary of Part 'A' and 'B' processes should help businesses decide whether or not any part of their operations comes under the Act. It is neither exhaustive nor detailed: if in doubt, check! Even if an aspect of an operation only seems close to an 'A' or 'B' process as described in general terms below, it may well still be covered – seek clarification: it is a summary rather than a definitive statement of law.

116

The list has also been drawn up on an *industry* basis in order to help businesses quickly identify themselves in the relevant category: the Act itself, though, is *process* based, concentrating (rightly) on the specific nature of potentially polluting operations rather than the broad industry category that they fall into. In most cases, the distinction doesn't matter: only oil companies, for example, are likely to find themselves unloading quantities of crude oil from tankers. Many businesses in all sorts of industries, on the other hand, are likely to find that they operate a waste incinerator – even if it's just an old dustbin or skip in the back yard. If so – it comes under Part 'B'!

PART 'A' AND PART 'B' PROCESSES

Part 'A' processes

1 Energy industries

- natural gas & liquified petroleum gas

- coal, lignite or other non-waste sources of gas

- gas turbines, boilers & furnaces (>50 MW thermal input)

- waste oil burners (>3 MW output)

2 Petroleum industry

- handling, storage refining & processing of:
  - crude oil
  - stabilised crude petroleum
  - crude shale oil
  - associated gases

117

3 Metals industries

- iron and steel cupolas (>7 tonnes holding capacity)

- electric furnaces (holding capacity >7 tonnes)

- iron ore processing & handling

- related foundry processes:
  - mould manufacture
  - fettling
  - grinding
  - shot-blasting

- slag processing

- aluminium, copper, brass & zinc (>7 tonnes holding capacity)

- zinc or tin mining

- processing of cadmium, mercury, beryllium & selenium & others eg magnesium, chromium etc

- processing of alloys containing set levels of the above

4 Minerals, glass, asbestos and cement industries

- cement manufacture

- lime slaking

- asbestos processing

- production of specified products containing asbestos

- manufacture of glass fibre

118

- firing of heavy clay & refractory goods

- vapour & salt glazing

5 Chemical industries

- manufacture and/or use of:
  - boat hull coatings
  - certain textile coatings
  - printing ink, paint or other coating, resulting in
  - special wastes in excess of 1000 tonnes/year
  - hexachlorobenzene-based dyestuffs

- manufacture and/or use of organic chemicals:
  - styrene
  - vinyl chloride
  - acetylene
  - aldehyde
  - amine
  - isocyanate
  - any organic sulphur compound
  - any phenol

- carbon disulphide
- any pyridine, methyl pyridine or di-methyl pyridine
- any organo-metallic compound
- any acrylate

■ acids and acid-using processes:
- sulphuric or oleum
- oxides of sulphur
- nitric acid
- phosphoric acid

■ halogens:
- fluorine
- chlorine
- bromine
- iodine

■ inorganic chemical processes:
- antimony
- arsenic
- beryllium
- gallium
- indium
- lead
- palladium
- platinum
- selenium
- tellurium
- thallium
- chromium
- magnesium
- manganese
- nickel
- zinc

119

■ fertiliser manufacture & granulation

■ pesticide production

■ pharmaceutical production (>25,000 tonnes/year)

■ paper pulp production
di-isocyanate processes

■ tar and bitumen (>5 tonnes/year)

6 Waste industries

■ burning of chemical & plastic manufacturing waste

■ incineration of chemicals:
  – bromine
  – cadmium
  – chlorine
  – fluorine
  – iodine
  – lead
  – mercury
  – nitrogen
  – phosphorous
  – sulphur
  – zinc

■ any waste in an incinerator with capacity >1 tonne/hour

■ chemical recovery

■ production of fuel from waste

7 Timber industries

■ certain treatment or curing processes for timber or wooden products

■ wood preserving, if giving rise to special waste levels in excess of 500 tonnes/year

Part 'B' processes

1 Chemical industries

- ink manufacture (organic solvent based)

- paint manufacture

- solvent and oil recovery

- use of di-isocyanates in manufacturing

- adhesive manufacture

2 Printing and coating industries

- print works

- fabric coating

- coil coating

- adhesive coating

- vehicle coating

- vehicle respraying

- metal container coating

3 Energy and fuel industries

- waste oil burners (<3 MW output)

- gas turbines (<50 & >20 MW thermal input)

- coal size reduction or regrading

- compression engines
  boilers (<50 & >20 MW thermal input)

4 Metals industries

- iron and steel cupolas (<7 tonnes holding capacity)

121

- electric furnaces (holding capacity <7 tonnes)

- related foundry processes:
  - mould manufacture
  - fettling
  - grinding
  - shot-blasting

- scrap metal recovery

- galvanising

- aluminium, copper, brass & zinc (<7 tonnes holding capacity)

- jewellery

5 Minerals, glass, asbestos and cement industries

122

- cement packing

- soda lime silica glass

- borosilicate glass

- fluoride opal glass

- lead glass

- glass polishing

- manufacture of coarse ceramics:
  - refractory bricks
  - stoneware pipes
  - facing & floor bricks
  - roof tiles

- lime slaking (not at lime works)

- manufacture of asbestos products

- size reduction and grading of minerals other than coal

6 Waste industries

- clinical waste incineration (hospital incinerators)
- manufacture of refuse derived fuel
- waste incinerators (<1 tonne/hour & >25 kg per hour)
- container burning

7 Animal industries (offensive trades)

- animal rendering
- fish meal manufacture
- maggot breeding
- skins and hides
- animal dealers
- animal feed manufacture
- edible byproducts processing

8 Timber industries

- timber manufacture
- timber treatment (chemicals)
- particle board manufacture

123

IDENTIFYING AND LICENSING POLLUTING PROCESSES

Many managers, on reading this list, will be tempted to breathe a sigh of relief. Others will have alarm bells ringing, whilst some businesses will be less certain. The list, it must be stressed, is only a guide, intended to provide a business's environmental audit team with a useful starting point. Despite this, its fairly extensive scope will doubtless leave many managers surprised at the number of seemingly innocuous activities covered – especially those listed as falling under Part 'B' coverage.

Nevertheless, on reading through it, businesses will have a rough idea of how urgently their audit teams need to review potential areas of non-compliance. Obvious questions of fact arise: does our business actually use listed chemicals – or not? What is the megawatt rating of our incinerators? (Hint: companies may find that the records they keep under COSSH regulations contain some of this information.) A good starting point for a business's audit team seeking clarification of the exact provisions of the Act is to get a copy of it – contact your nearest HMSO shop. The Department of the Environment publishes useful guidance notes on Part 'A' and Part 'B' of the Environmental Protection Act. These are well worth getting.

124

In some cases, there will be information gaps that need filling before the degree of compliance can be established. A business may be unaware of the exact contents and quantities of its wastes – although the waste-reduction checklist in Chapter 4 will hopefully have got the identification process underway. Clearly, though, some waste is unavoidable, and managers need to be very clear about what it comprises, and what the disposal process for it is. If it includes substances listed in the Act, is the disposal contractor aware of this? Is the site that he uses to dispose of it actually licensed as being permitted to take it? This is where the 'duty of care' provision of the Act comes in.

But there are other, less obvious wastes. The audit questions in Chapter 4 focused (although not exclusively) on measurable quantities of wastes that had to be positively disposed of. However, the Act also covers less tangible wastes such as smoke and dust arising as byproducts of manufacturing processes. It is here, in fact, that Part 'B' of the Act bites hardest – as we have seen, perfectly ordinary businesses, not normally regarded in any way as noxious, are now, for probably the first time, being asked to consider their manufacturing process as environment polluting. The printing shop, the vehicle resprayers, the brickworks, the small back street foundry – all these are now Part 'B' polluters.

As such, they – and all other Part 'B' businesses – are obliged to obtain prior authorisation to operate. As the last of the three-staged deadlines for application passed in September 1992 in England and Wales (March 1993 in Scotland) businesses without local authority approval are now operating outside the law. Thousands of businesses are therefore not only finding themselves defined as Part 'B' polluters, but also as *illegal* Part 'B' polluters. They are liable for fines which maybe unlimited, and up to two years' imprisonment – so not surprisingly, the advice that has been offered to Part 'B' businesses finding themselves in such a situation is to take legal advice as quickly as possible. (In the case of any Part 'A' businesses reading this, contact HMIP.)

125

But even for these businesses, the consequences of the Act coming into force are far more than a one-off scramble to catch up and become legal. The Act is an *ongoing* commitment in two distinct senses. Firstly, businesses themselves change – growing in size, moving premises and expanding product lines to take advantage of new opportunities. Businesses quite outside the scope of Part 'A' or 'B' at the moment may thus find themselves affected by a change in their operations. 'Are we contemplating doing anything that would takes us into the scope of the Act?' needs to become part of a firm's regular review process.

The second aspect of the ongoing nature of the Act is because businesses are constantly changing the way that they do things. Manufacturing processes change, with new ways of making things coming in, and plant and equipment being updated and replaced. An approval under the Act to operate a specific process is not a carte blanche: it is a permit to operate the particular process that was licensed. A significant change to the process may require a fresh application. Furthermore, BATNEEC itself changes and evolves: an acceptable process today may be unacceptable tomorrow, as newer and cleaner technology becomes available. A thorough understanding of the implications of the Act is vital.

Applications to operate a process that falls under the Act must be in writing, and need to contain information covering five aspects of the operation:

- details of the operator and the location of the process;

- a description of the process and the techniques employed to prevent or minimise the emission to the atmosphere of prescribed substances, and to render any such emissions harmless;

- details of the source, nature and amount of current and/or anticipated air emissions from the process;

- proposals for monitoring, sampling and measurement of air emissions;

- assessment of the likely consequences of any emissions to air.

Nor is that all. In certain circumstances, additional information will be required. These comprise instances where:

- there are a number of alternative means of minimising emissions to the air, each one having a different environmental impact;

- the applicant proposes to depart significantly from the advice contained in the Secretary of State's process guidance notes – these have been produced as an adjunct to the Act;

- a process is (or will be) located in or near to a sensitive environmental area – such as in a town centre, or upwind of a Site of Special Scientific Interest;

- a process is, or will be, located in an area with already high pollution levels, so that the additional proposed pollution will cause total levels to approach or exceed statutory air quality standards.

Each application for authorisation carries a fee of up to £800 – and a business may need to make several for different processes on the same site, and for different sites. General guidance notes, and the more specific Secretary of State's process guidance notes are available from the Department of the Environment. These do give clear advice on making an application, but there is nothing to stop applicants from holding prior informal discussions with HMIP or their local authority first, to minimise the possibility of rejection.

127

Key to success is the application of technology to minimise emissions. But by how much? The answer, as we saw earlier, lies in BATNEEC: the best available techniques not entailing excessive cost. The Department of the Environment's interpretation of BATNEEC is clearly worth noting.

Best: 'must be taken to mean the most effective in preventing, minimising or rendering harmless polluting emissions. There may be more than one set of techniques that achieves comparable effectiveness – that is, there may be more than one set of best techniques.'

Available: 'should be taken to mean procurable by the operator of the process in question. It does not imply that the technique is in general use, but does require general accessibility. It includes a technique which has been developed at a scale which allows its implementation in the relevant industrial context with the necessary business confidence. It does not imply that sources outside the UK are unavailable. Nor does it imply a competitive supply market. If there is a monopoly supplier the technique counts as available provided that the operator can secure it.'

Techniques: 'embraces both the process and how it is operated. It should be taken to mean the concept and the design of the process, the components of which it is made up and the manner in which they are connected together to make the whole. It also includes matters such as numbers and qualifications of staff, working methods, training and supervision and also the design, construction, layout and maintenance of buildings.'

NEEC: 'Not Entailing Excessive Cost should be taken in two contexts, depending on whether it is applied to new or existing processes. For new processes, the presumption should be that best available techniques are used, but, in the Secretary of State's view, that presumption can be properly modified by economic considerations where the costs of applying best available techniques would be excessive in relation to the nature of the industry and the environmental protection to be achieved. In relation to existing processes, each of the Secretary of State's process guidance notes specify timescales over which old processes should be upgraded to new standards, or decommissioned.'

Once a local authority has received an application, it should decide within two weeks if it 'is duly made' – that is, if it contains everything that is required in order for a decision to be reached. If not, further information may be sought by the authority. The business can appeal if this would involve the release of information that could be commercially confidential – which may be quite likely, perhaps, in the case of new processes. However, even if such an appeal is allowed, full publication may still have to be made after four years.

Once all the information that is required has been submitted, the authority is obliged to place an advertisement in the local press, rather like the advertisements placed following certain planning applications. This essentially summarises the contents of the application, and makes the public aware that such an application has been made. The authority is also obliged to send copies of the application to bodies such as the Health and Safety Executive. Normally, it should notify the business of its decision on the application within four months. In some circumstances this can be quite a significant time delay – such as during the decision process surrounding a piece of potentially competition-killing new investment. Yet again, this underscores the advisability of approaching authorities early and on an informal basis first.

129

Once approval has been granted, a business may operate the particular process that has been licensed. It is also required to monitor the emissions from it on an ongoing basis, and to retain and submit monitoring records to meet the terms of their authorisations and licences.

Beyond Part I of the Environmental Protection Act

So where next? How far does business' legal responsibility with respect to pollution extend beyond the provisions contained in Part I of the Environmental Protection Act? And what about its additional ethical obligations – are there other areas of potential pollution, as yet unregulated, that firms need to think about?

Unsurprisingly, the answer in both cases is 'yes'! In exploring further, though, we advance much more into greyer and greyer areas. Not that even Part I of the Environmental Protection Act is black and white. As with any pioneering piece of legislation, only time, and case law, can fully bring out the answers to questions of interpretation and practice. These are already starting to emerge. Who really has the final say on BATNEEC? Can firms be relied upon to effectively monitor their own emissions – and if not, who should do it instead? Are the various schedules of listed substances and processes extensive enough? With the ink on the Act barely dry, pressure groups on both sides of the fence were already squabbling and finding fault.

A business carrying out an environmental audit is therefore in an awkward position. And sadly, one of the Act's major supposed benefits to the business community has yet to really materialise. The Act, as originally envisaged, was supposed to bring in – through the concept of integrated pollution control – a sort of environmental 'one-stop shopping'. The quid pro quo, if such there was, amounted to settling for a tougher legislative regime in exchange for a simpler administrative framework. That arguably has yet to emerge: businesses still find themselves needing to deal with a number of bodies – HMIP, their local authority, the National Rivers Authority and so on. Compliance with multiple requirements replaces the hoped for – and simpler – compliance with a single set of clearly stated rules. Instead of focusing their attention on the Act and *beyond* it, businesses are still having to look *backwards*, at the decades of disparate rules and regulations from which it emerged.

Predictably, compliance is patchy. The principal problem is probably ignorance: few business people actively *want* to pollute – but there are so many potential contaminants, and so many ways in which they can escape into the environment. Take the typical factory yard: goods are loaded and unloaded (with spillages, in the nature of things, bound to occur from time to time), and vehicles parked, washed or possibly even repaired. Yet who asks where the drains go? A cocktail of detergent, oil, lead and chemicals is washed down them every time it rains or vehicles are washed. Theory: areas draining to surface water should be demarcated, so that certain activities don't take place there. Fact: few businesses bother – or even know that they need to.

There are legislative gaps, too. A business using solvents, benzenes, volatile organic compounds and the like may or may not be required to register under Part 'B' of Part I of the Act. But lots of businesses use solvents – and not just manufacturing or engineering businesses: a bottle of typing correction fluid sits on many a secretary's desk, and plenty of offices have bottles of general purpose solvent for cleaning purposes.

131

An audit checklist

Despite this hotchpotch, the green business has to do *something*. The audit checklist that follows tries to reflect a business's legal obligations as well as sensible good practice. The assumption behind it is not that a business, having worked through it, has a 'clean bill of health'; but that working through it ought to give the typical business enough to be going on with. It is also (of necessity) a fairly generalised sort of list: experts at your industry or trade association (as discussed in Chapter 3) should be able to provide the more specific advice that is applicable to your business. Talk to HMIP, your local council, your waste regulation authority and the National Rivers Authority – they all give statutory advice. But start your audit off with the following:

1 Is your business a Part 'A' or Part 'B' business under Part I of the Environmental Protection Act? This is not necessarily a straightforward question to answer. A business will be aware of whether or not it manufactures clay pipes (say), but some probing may well be necessary to ascertain the use or otherwise of any of the listed chemical compounds or alloys. Hint: don't forget to include in the deliberations not just the main product lines and processes, but the minor lines and 'specially coated' variants or the like that might be produced. The main product line may well have no licensing implication at all under the Act – it could be the coating that contains the relevant substance. Again, talk to the applicable trade or industry association.

2 Many straightforward raw materials and finished products will be contaminating pollutants if released into the environment in inappropriate ways or quantities. Businesses typically store large quantities of both – and accidents happen. Be concerned not just about potential hazards to humans, but also plants and wildlife. Check:

(i) The legal requirements concerning the storage of potentially hazardous materials.

(ii) That storage areas are contained or 'bunded' to prevent run-off etc in the case of accidents, flooding or fire. (In the case of *waste*, this is a legal requirement.)

(iii) Loading and unloading procedures – are they as accident-proof as possible? How much manhandling of drums etc is involved?

(iv) Contingency plans are in place to deal with any spillages, accidents or fires that *do* occur. Remember, once, no one had heard of Seveso, Chernobyl etc. Now, thanks in part to shortcomings in their control systems and contingency planning, no one will forget them.

(v) Plans might be in place – but are staff trained in implementing them? People move on, and a scruffy scrap of paper stuck to a noticeboard, forgotten in the heat of the moment, is no substitute for a rehearsed and practised procedure that people are familiar with.

(vi) Could business concepts such as 'Just in Time', where goods are delivered by suppliers more or less as they are required, cut down on the amount of environmentally hazardous material stored on site?

3 Part II of the Environmental Protection Act imposes in particular a duty of care upon businesses in respect of their waste, as well as penalties for improper dealing in waste.

(i) Are wastes clearly labelled, packaged and segregated?

133

(ii) Are accurate records maintained of the wastes that have been generated – and the disposal routes used to remove them?

(iii) Analyse these routes: do they meet applicable legal requirements – or, in their absence, any published recommendations? Overall, do they minimise potential environmental damage?

(iv) In the case of businesses employing waste disposal contractors, do the contractors know precisely what is in the waste that they are removing? Are they legally licensed? Have their premises been visited? Are their provisions for dealing with it appropriate? Most importantly – is there on file documentation from them to support this?

4 Emissions and discharges into the environment, not directly attributable to waste, will inevitably arise from your operations. Evaporation, spillage, leaching, dust – all are possible escape routes. So:

(i) What escapes – and how? Look at *all* routes – accidental spillage and leakage, as well as drying, coating, cleaning operations.

(ii) Where do the drains go – and what goes down them? Is anything other than surface water run-off going into surface water drains · don't forget the impact of vehicle operations referred to earlier. Don't just consider substances presently known to be harmful to humans – look at escapes of *anything* into the environment.

(iii) What can be done to minimise the use of 'no-no' substances, which whilst legal, are definitely non-green. Chemicals to start with (but then look at the fuller list in the Part 'A' and 'B' schedules on pages 117–123): any chlorinated compound, volatile organic compound, benzenes & other solvents. If their use *is* essential, make it as minimal as possible – and do all possible to prevent leakage to the environment – which includes evaporation: most of these are greenhouse gases.

(iv) List *all* your emissions. What are the legal requirements – and do you meet them? What are the 'best practice' levels? Do you meet these? Don't forget noise and odour. For any discharges to water, consent is required under the Water Resources Act.

134

The legacy of the past

Not many questions – but certainly a lot of work to find the answers. So – is it *really* necessary? Fine, say some, prevent greenhouse gases escaping into the atmosphere: that's sensible. Nor is there anything wrong with preventing obviously harmful chemicals entering the food chain. But isn't the rest of it slightly over the top? Are levels of land and water contamination really high enough to warrant the sort of action proposed above? It's a predictable enough question – and one that deserves an answer. But when contemplating the lengths to go to to counter contamination, consider the following.

There are, it is estimated, already between 50,000 and 100,000 significantly contaminated sites in the UK. Generally former factory, warehouse or mining sites, they date from a time when pollution controls were less strict than they are today, counter-technology more primitive and the consequences of contamin-ation not so clearly appreciated. The battery factory, lead works, chemical company, vehicle repairer or scrap metal merchant might have ceased trading or moved on years ago: the legacy of chemicals, lead, oil, solvent and metals – or what-ever else – that they have left behind lives on. Many businesses operate on such sites. Under the nicely landscaped industrial estate of today may lie the railway goods yard, docklands ware-house, inner-city factory or scrap metal merchants of bygone days.

135

A little-appreciated part of the Environmental Protection Act – Part VIII – places a duty on local authorities to identify possibly contaminated land that has been put to a number of listed uses and set up public registers of it. The gargantuan task has barely started: a figure of £600 million has been estimated as the cost of merely investigating – *not* cleaning – the 40,000 hectares identified in the 1988 Derelict Land Survey. And that's only land not presently in use. The cost of identifying contaminated land in active use, never mind starting to clean it up, is impossible to state, but will be enormous.

As the shape of these registers starts to emerge, it is slowly dawning on both businesses and their bankers that one of a firm's biggest assets – its site – may not be worth what is claimed on the balance sheet. It may even have a zero (or indeed negative) value: decontaminating polluted land is a costly exercise. Why do it all? Because the ultimate aim of the registers is to control subsequent use of contaminated land, and to make potential buyers – and neighbours – aware of the risks and dangers posed by particular sites. Undecontaminated land may be impossible to sell.

Scaremongering, maybe – and it is, at the time of writing, difficult to predict the exact ultimate reactions of organisations such as banks and local councils who are still really coming to terms with recognising the issue. One thing, though, seems certain: reaction is really a question of degree. The problem is not going to go away.

So: a closing thought for any business reading the foregoing chapter and thinking 'to hell with it' – or for any Board of Directors continuing to foul the land that it stands on because doing so is cheaper than doing anything about it. Your site may be your biggest asset – doesn't it make sense to protect its value?

136

7

Sharing the planet

This chapter looks beyond the business at its relationships with the whole biosphere – plants, wildlife and people. We examine:

- **why the biosphere matters**

- **how business activities affect it**

- **environmentally-friendly practices in the workplace**

- **audit checklists.**

All creatures great and small

And now for something completely different. Nor, as it happens, is the old *Monty Python* catchphrase an inappropriate way to start. This chapter is about our impact on the rest of the planet's biosphere – the animals, insects, fish, plants and birds that we share the Earth with. As we saw in Chapter 1, vast swathes of tropical rainforest have already gone. More is going – a further 170,000 square kilometres is cut back every year, an area equivalent to England, Wales and Northern Ireland. That's an awful lot of dead and displaced parrots – not to mention members of other species. For tropical rainforests, which cover only six per cent of the world's land surface, contain more than half of the species in the world.

The facts are bewildering. There are 2000 species of fish in the Amazon – that's ten times as many as in the whole of Europe.

There are more tree species in just ten hectares of rainforest in Borneo than in the whole of the continental United States. Though no one will ever know how many species there *were* in Brazil's rich Atlantic coastal rainforest: ninety-eight per cent of it has gone. Likewise in the Philippines, seventy-eight per cent of whose rainforest has disappeared – and continues to vanish. Despite logging controls, twice as many logs from the Philippines are (quite literally) smuggled into Japan as are legally exported there.

Once the trees are gone, the land that remains is subject to drought – and also soil erosion. Forests are great retainers and recyclers of water: land covered with woodland absorbs twenty times more rainwater than bare earth. Without it, the water just runs off – bringing flooding, erosion and impaired fertility. *With* forest cover, the water is absorbed, and gradually released, seeping out more slowly over a longer period. In India, the number of villages short of water in Uttar Pradesh – where there has been heavy logging – has risen from 17,000 to 70,000 in two decades. Forty per cent of the world's population rely on mountain range forest cover for stable water supplies.

138

There's more. As we saw in Chapter 1, science has identified unique and powerful medicines amongst those plants that it has so far looked at – and it has barely scratched the surface of the task. Scientists are still trying to simply *count* the number of species: around 1.4 million of the estimated thirty million species on the planet have so far been catalogued. It will be centuries before the job is finished, and centuries more before many are studied in detail – assuming that they are still around. And let's hope so – because the rewards from them can be rich. Take the Madagascan rosy periwinkle, which contains two unique and powerful drugs used in the treatment of leukaemia and Hodgkin's disease. From the threatened Pacific Yew comes taxol, a recently identified treatment for cancer –

ovarian and breast tumours which respond to no other treatment are successfully attacked by it. Nor should our motives be wholly selfish. The world would be immensely poorer if species like tigers were allowed to vanish – as they have come very close to doing. Even today, the Earth's tiger population still only numbers around 7500.

But the environment is much more than a remote place on the other side of the planet, full of zoological exotica. In fact, the environment starts right outside your business's back door – and its biosphere includes all the plants and animals whose habitats and lives are impacted by your business, whether they are in Borneo or Birmingham. For British woodlands and forests have been devastated, too. The land covered by ancient forests is now only one per cent of what it once was. Policies of re-afforestation have often produced only ugly plantations of conifers. Twenty-eight per cent of UK plantation tree cover is now in fact an alien import – the North American sitka spruce. Though the timber resources that come from such plantations are at least better than indiscriminate logging of natural woodlands, they are far from perfect. Generally comprising densely packed pine or spruce trees of the same species, they form unwelcoming habitats for birds, insects and woodland plantlife. Traditional broadleaved forests and woodlands, with their mixtures of tree species – oak, ash, birch, chestnut and the like – are far greener, in both senses of the term.

The biosphere also includes *you*, and the rest of your business's workforce, and those of its customers and suppliers as well as the general public. For we also share the planet with ourselves – and with those generations that will follow us. Policies and practices injurious to wildlife (whether positively or passively) are rarely healthy for humans either, although the side effects may take far longer to show up.

The central theme of this chapter is a simple one: it explores ways of making the impact that your business has on the biosphere as green a one as possible. It differs from the previous chapters in two key respects. Firstly, the focus is diffuse – far more so than (say) with energy conservation or pollution. Normally, this would make a subject heavy going, but thankfully this is not the case. For the second key difference between this chapter and others is the extent to which the environmental argument is essentially over. Few people need persuading about the *need* to be environmentally responsible in this area – it is generally a case of pushing at an open door, and an already fairly green one at that. Energy conservation, as an issue to get excited about, is far less accessible. Fuel is affordable and still relatively abundant, and the side effects of its use both invisible and relatively long term. Energy conservation is an absolutely crucial environmental issue – yet is still one that many people need persuading about.

Not so preserving the biosphere. Many people have a genuine affinity for plants and wildlife, and – directly at least – are often upset at sights of animal suffering. The problem comes where the linkage is not a direct one – and it is here that the acceptance of the need to be environmentally responsible is not matched by corresponding actions. People grieve for the floundering sea birds following an oil spillage – such as the Exxon *Valdez*, off the Alaskan coastline in 1989, or the more recent *Braer* disaster off the Shetlands in 1993 – but do little about turning down their heating, or altering their transportation methods. The indirect consequences of their choice of timber, packaging or foodstuffs are equally injurious – and also more widespread. Again, the link is not appreciated as strongly as it should be, although this is changing.

Another link that is firming up in people's minds is that that exists between being environmentally responsible and being in good health. Substances that are harmful to the plants and animals that we share the biosphere with are not likely to be without effect upon humans – although such effects may be slow in action, and remote from their original point of use. Chemical sprays and liquids used with such abandon years ago are now subject to tight controls and strict regulations covering protective clothing and the like – although for some people, this is sadly too late. Nowadays, many of the obvious hazards have been minimised through legislation: Health and Safety at Work regulations and factory inspectors control the worst excesses of yesteryear industrial practice. The Environmental Protection Act plays its part too, limiting the amounts of airborne dust and smoke that employees can subsequently inhale.

Yet many workplaces remain unhealthy and 'user hostile' places. 'Sick building' syndrome, poor (artificial) lighting, noise, stress and employee cafeterias – all play their part in contributing to unwholesome work environments that lead to unwell and ultimately unproductive employees. Especially in predominantly office-type business activities, the impact of workplace catering will be high on the business's green agenda. Here, process pollution and similar industrially-related issues are of far less relevance than the environmental impact of the office canteen. It's easy for the audit team to look at the mass of coffee machines, the throwaway plastic cups, plates, cutlery, the 'one-shot' UHT milk portions and so forth and see opportunities for waste reduction, energy efficiency and more recycling. It's harder for them to explore the environmental consequences of the food and drink itself – although, as we shall see, the maxim 'what's good for people is good for the environment' is an excellent rule of thumb.

141

We have touched on the *differences* between this and the other chapters: the diffuse nature of some of the issues, and the extent to which discussion of them is 'pushing at an open door'. There are also similarities. Key amongst these is again the interconnectedness of the arguments: recycling, better energy efficiency, not polluting, cutting out waste – these are all policies that also lead to a greener relationship with our habitat.

So the business that has worked its way through the audit process to this point has already done much to make its interaction with the biosphere greener. Fewer tanker loads of oil or truckloads of coal will be required, fewer pollutants will reach rivers and fields and fewer natural habitats will be destroyed by landfill or logging. But there *is* more that can be done. Let's now turn to examine two further lines of questioning for the business's audit team to probe:

- What are the environmental interactions with the biosphere that need considering in conjunction with some of the points that we've looked at earlier? Take timber purchases, for example. After eliminating waste, and doing all that they can to reclaim and reuse, businesses will find that some new timber will still inevitably be required. What environmental considerations does the green business observe in its purchase of it?

- We have looked in previous chapters at those major environmental issues that, as we saw in Chapter 2, generally fall to businesses rather than individuals. But how can businesses add a green dimension to other parts of their activities? What do they have to do in order to be responsible green employers and consumers?

Business and the biosphere: audit checklist

1 Businesses buy a vast range of 'consumables' – products that don't directly go into the products that they make or sell, but help in running the business. Stationery, cleaning liquids, paints and so on. So:

(i)   A few individuals in a Purchasing Department can have an enormous influence on a business's buying practices. How environmentally minded are the people in yours? Have they been asked to be?

(ii) Does the Purchasing Department seek out and ask for products with an identifying 'green' tag? Many are already marked this way, others are coming on stream. Does it check that the claims made for products are reasonable and that they are genuinely green? A product is not automatically green just because it has 'recyclable' stamped on it! Things to start with:

- Washing-up liquid – how many bottles does your business buy each year? 'Green' liquids are biodegradable and made of natural substances

- Likewise many other cleaning products – see section on catering below

- Toilet rolls

- Continuous computer and laser printer paper

- Office stationery – photocopying paper, 'letterhead' paper, envelopes and filing products.

All sorts of claims are made for paper and paper products. 'Recycled' (the ideal) *ought* to mean, as we saw in Chapter 4, post-consumer recycled waste – as opposed to paper industry recycled waste. So:

- Check the post-consumer waste content of any recycled papers that you buy.

143

- Encourage the use of one hundred per cent *non-bleached* recycled paper for internal use eg photo-copying & memos. It doesn't look as nice – but it *is* just about as green as you can get.

(iii) Other people within organisations buy or specify products – such as from office supply catalogues and the like. Are they looking out for green products as well? Has a policy statement been circulated, encouraging this? What are individuals supposed to decide when the green product costs five per cent more? Or ten per cent more? (Not that it should: make sure everyone is briefed on the arguments in Chapter 2 – going green isn't an excuse for being ripped off by unscrupulous suppliers . . .)

(iv) Do products that you use contain environmentally injurious substances? If so, can you purchase greater alternatives instead? This helps minimise potential pollution and environmental damage to the biosphere further back in the supply chain – and reduces the overall impact of your business on the environment. For if businesses are not buying such products, other businesses won't be sup-plying them. Some of those in the list below are also implicated in 'Sick Building Syndrome' – another good reason for avoiding them. Especially avoid:

- Volatile Organic Compounds such as benzene, toluene, propane, butane etc. These are found in paints, polishes and cleaning solvents.

- Wood preservatives or combined staining treatments containing lindane, tributynoxide or tetrachlorophenol.

- Pesticides containing 2,4,5–T, which is banned in a number of countries.

- CFCs, used as aerosol propellants and in refrigerators, freezers and cooling systems.

- Halons – found in firefighting systems.

2 Are you buying, or about to buy, products based on non-green exploitation of the biosphere?

(i) Businesses are prodigious consumers of tropical hardwoods. They are expensive – but managers and directors can take the view it's not their own money that they are spending. Encouraged by concepts such as 'image' they can inadvertently actually *demand* exceptionally non-green products! Look around you, or think about those parts of your business premises visited by customers, or used by senior managers and directors. Are tables, chairs or panelling made of mahogany, teak, or other tropical hardwoods? Or even English oak? The attractive leather seat coverings – exactly what sort of animal did it come from? How much of the money paid for them actually went to people in the Third World? (Typically, this figure is around only ten per cent of the price paid by the ultimate Western purchaser.) So:

145

(a) Specify that purchases of wooden furniture, doors etc must come from *sustainably grown and harvested* forests and woodlands.

(b) Try and buy products where as much value as possible has been added in the country of origin.

(c) Avoid exotic leather coverings or fur trimmings.

3 Is your business a green employer? There is a difference between legal Health and Safety at Work requirements and green best practice: quite ordinary materials may be harmful given prolonged exposure in sufficient quantity.

(i) Do you observe the minimum legal safety levels on substance handling or the maximum possible? What is best practice in your industry? What does your trade association actually recommend? Consider:

■ Protective clothing

- Gloves

- Eye protection

- Dust masks

- Automating handling & dispensing

(ii)   Are employees positively encouraged to work safely – or do pressures of work (and payment systems) encourage people to take short cuts?

(iii) Do you have a no-smoking policy? Is smoking discouraged, or allowed only in certain areas? Tobacco smoke pollutes the air, and is injurious to non-smokers, one of whom dies per day in the UK through inhaling other people's smoke.

<u>146</u>   **4** Does your business actively encourage green practices? Is it *seen* to be a green employer and corporate citizen?

(i)   Have you adopted the 1992 environmental management standard, BS7750? (See next chapter for details of it.)

(ii)   Do you know which of your suppliers have?

(iii) Are you encouraging those that haven't to do so – and switching away from those that won't?

(iv)   Look searchingly at your site and the impact it has on its surroundings. Think about:

- Litter (don't forget – also covered by the Environmental Protection Act!)

- Unattractive, dirty or faded exterior appearance that looks tatty and doesn't blend in with the surroundings – especially important in rural and semi-rural areas.

- Poorly maintained buildings and exterior fittings. Premature replacement of rusted or rotten materials is non-green.

- Derelict wasteland – could it be turned into lawn or parkland with some amenity or natural habitat value?

- Piles of junked machinery, drums (and any contents that may remain in them), old pallets and the like.

(v) Are employees actively encouraged to be green, and to consider the impact of their actions on the environment? (There's more on establishing this 'green culture' in the next chapter.) Look for:

- A green Policy Statement – do people know what the business's views on the environment are? Are they even aware that the business *has* any views?

- Are employees encouraged to submit green contributions to the suggestion scheme – and what happens to them? How are they judged?

147

- Active employee participation in recycling and reclaiming of materials via segregated bins and containers – 'grass roots' involvement is important. Large scale interception of material for recycling is one thing – getting people to separate out the recyclable materials from the mass of paper, drinks can and so on that go into the typical office bin is quite another.

- Likewise energy consciousness at the individual level – are people switching lights off, and *really* cutting down on unnecessary ventilation, heating and transport?

5 Any business's catering offers lots of opportunities to be green. Some we've looked at in earlier chapters – washable mugs instead of throwaway cups, recycling of kitchen wastes and so on. But also look at the scope for:

(i) Environmentally friendly cleaning agents – dishwasher powders, washing-up liquids, surface cleaners and hand soaps. Look for products which carry reputable green labelling. Whilst plenty of equivalent consumer products in

the supermarket carry such labelling – because of consumer pressure – catering packs and products have yet to
catch up. Again, consumers can exercise that choice in the
supermarket because they see actual products available:
your catering staff may simply order the same non-green
brand time after time. Issues to be aware of:

(a) Re-fillable containers and returnable/recyclable
packaging.

(b) Purchase only soaps that haven't been tested on
animals. You know the burning sensation when soap
gets in your eyes? That's what some tests on rabbits
involve.

(c) Some dishwasher powders use phosphates and
bleaches – try not to use them.

148

(ii) Food can be green, too. Company canteens were once
bywords for institutional catering at its worst – stodge,
overcooked vegetables, and a 'meat and two veg'
mentality. The switch to contract caterers has brought a
breath of fresh air to all this, as has a switch in people's
dietary habits and expectations. Nevertheless, there's still
lots of scope left. Points to watch out for:

(a) Meat isn't very green – for several reasons. Land used
for cattle rearing could support up to sixteen times as
many people if it was used for growing crops. *Plus*:
people often think that cattle are raised exclusively on
grass – they're not. Over half the world's grain crop
goes to feed cattle – on around a ten per cent con-
version efficiency. A whole sack of grain is required to
produce 5½ lbs of meat. Amazingly, over half of the
Brazilian rainforest has been cut down to form
pastureland for cattle raising. Offering some alternatives to meat – such as fish, egg- or bean-based dishes
is both greener and healthier.

(b) Fried eggs, scrambled eggs, omelets – your catering budget will almost certainly include a lot of eggs. Do you specify free range? Battery farming is cruel and unnatural in a number of ways.

(c) Do you use as much fresh produce as possible? Try to minimise the use of frozen, preserved or ready processed produce. Do the recipes that you use follow the seasons as much as possible? It's an alien concept these days, to be sure, but is the greenest and most natural policy.

(d) Do your catering staff specify organically grown foodstuffs wherever possible? Non-organically grown food is exposed to additives and chemical sprays and treatments.

(e) Do you serve wholefoods, salads, fruit and vegetarian dishes? If not, could you? Would people eat them? Try re-educating employees' tastebuds – and remember, the people who *do* want these foods may well be the very people (such as the younger, more diet-conscious ones) who may not be using the catering facilities at the moment.

149

Staying vigilant

The world changes – and so do businesses. We've looked in this chapter at some major problems, and listed the sort of audit issues faced by typical businesses. As such, the focus has been on businesses' day-to-day concerns. Businesses do occasionally move and relocate – the environmental issues facing them then are totally different, and outside the scope of this book. Seeking specialist help is one solution, and commercial organisations do exist that will offer such advice.

In practice, exercising a little care, consideration and common sense goes a long way. A business is essentially tied to the environmental implications of much of its existing building and landscaping – a new one offers a fresh start. Try to minimise the disruption to wildlife in the construction phase, and to avoid disturbing natural habits – especially during the breeding and nesting phases. Try to incorporate what's already on the land into your designs, rather than just designing on the assumption of a flat featureless piece of ground. Retain ponds, streams and trees. Car parks as 'bays' set in amongst landscaped banks, with bushes and trees, not only look better, but preserves homes for wildlife. Building on reclaimed derelict land is better than building on a green field site.

150

The building itself obviously offers a fresh start in terms of issues of energy efficiency and pollution. But there are also opportunities in relation to the biosphere. Where does the timber come from? Avoid wood that doesn't come from sustainably managed woodlands – and especially resist the temptation to incorporate another panelled boardroom just like your last one. If you have to have one – get contractors to dismantle your old panelling and reinstall it in the new building. This probably means having an architect design your new room around the dimensions of your existing one, but is worth it.

Relocating or not, any business will see new issues, not covered in this book, emerge – areas such as energy efficiency or pollution tend to be rather more static in nature than biosphere-related environmental concerns. So try to keep abreast of them. Follow the press – subscribe to the periodical of an environmental pressure group. *Join* an environmental pressure group. And ask employees to help keep in touch: we look in the next chapter at ways of harnessing people and getting them involved in environmental issues.

8

Going for green

We now turn to the business of actually getting things done. The audit has shown us where we are – now let's look at the issues involved in moving forward. This chapter looks at:

■ developing an environmental action plan

■ environmental statements and reporting

■ the role of BS7750

■ helping the green cause.

Getting underway

And so to implementation. The audit process will inevitably have produced a mixed bag of findings – some areas of environmental concern being inappropriate, some highly relevant but broadly complied with, and others relevant but virtually untouched.

The business, once the audit is complete, will have to take a view about the overall level of compliance in order to determine a sensible way forward. Is there a lot to do – or a little? Is it urgent, or can a rolling programme be developed to tackle things on, say, a five year basis? Managements will understandably be loath to scrap or rebuild process equipment and machinery that is virtually new, but will regard building in environmentally friendly features into new purchases in a more favourable light. Some things, too, are easier to get started on than others. Starting off down the road towards recycling is something most businesses can do virtually immediately – but gets harder later on, as the firm moves on from basic recycling of paper and plastics into more ambitious areas. Energy efficiency, too, starts off simply – wastes of energy, once identified, are relatively easy to prevent. The fine tuning takes a little longer.

So a start needs making – but how? And by whom? And where to stop – for what are the business's objectives? This chapter looks at these issues, but also one or two rather broader ones. There is now an environmental management British Standard – BS7750. What does it cover – and should businesses adopt it? How should the firm measure and monitor its activities with respect to the environment? And what can the business do to help the environmental *movement* – as opposed to the environment itself?

Developing an environmental action plan

The first step is to determine the business's *policy* towards the environment. The lengths the business goes to to achieve this will probably be dictated by its size and the nature of the activities and the activities that it carries out. Massive petrochemical complexes will pursue different – more demanding and detailed – policies to those deemed necessary by smaller businesses. Some organisations need to go into tremendous depth, others don't.

The policy is principally there for three purposes:

1 To act as a statement of intent – something that the business can adopt as a guiding principle or mission. Having made it –

it can break it. But the idea is that at least if it's set down, temptation will prove slightly easier to resist.

2 To let the outside world know the business's views and intentions on the environment. As the law tightens up on environmental abuse, firms may find themselves bound to have an environmental policy, much as they increasingly find themselves required to report to outside parties their Health and Safety and Quality policies.

3 To communicate to its own people what its views are. People come and go in organisations, and rules and dictats get forgotten or overlooked in the heat of day-to-day decision making. A written policy acts as a constant reminder.

What precisely a business puts in its policy will vary from business to business. Typically, though, a basic policy might contain items such as these:

153

- The directors, senior management and all employees are committed to the following environmental policy:

- To set environmental guidelines and standards that at the very least meet national and local statutory requirements.

- To review and develop these guidelines and standards in the light of developments in technology and industrial practices, and of trends in legislation.

- To minimise waste and to re-use and recycle materials and products.

- To improve energy use through conservation measures and increased energy efficiency.

- To minimise or eliminate the use of toxic materials and chemicals.

- To assess the actual and potential environmental effects of all existing or planned products and projects.

- To inform all employees of their responsibilities in implementation of your company's environmental guidelines and standards, and to ensure that appropriate training and resources are provided to ensure that they are implemented effectively

- To carry out monitoring, through environmental audits, for example, to ensure that your company's environmental guidelines and standards are being met.

- To ensure that contractors and suppliers working with your company are informed of and comply with your company's environmental guidelines and standards.

- To make available information about your company's environmental guidelines and standards to all stakeholders, including the local community, who have an interest in your company and its environmental performance.

154

Nothing desperately radical there – and note the use of words like 'minimise' and 'improve'. But achieving even these modest objectives will call for a fair amount of hard work. It is almost certain that a comparison of policy with actual practice, as revealed by the audit, will yield a number of gaps that need closing.

Fortunately, at least part of the closure mechanism is likely to be in place already. For these are changing – and challenging – times for business. Management are increasingly faced with finding themselves having to respond to multiple initiatives . . . Total Quality, Just in Time, Customer Service Excellence, adopting the BS5750 quality standard, COSHH, Health and Safety Regulations and so on. For all these initiatives, businesses will have already been exposed to the problems and difficulties associated with building up a plan to achieve something, and then nailing down precisely who is going to do exactly what. The bad news is that you'll have to go through the same process once again, if you want to achieve anything much more substantial than an office waste paper collection. The good news, though, is that it may well turn out to be slightly easier than hitherto.

Stakeholders in a business – customers, employees, directors, shareholders, local residents or whoever – are generally sympathetic to environmental initiatives. As we've said previously, few people particularly *want* to despoil the planet – it just happens, as other goals are pursued. Accordingly, implementing actions to protect the environment need not be as difficult as (say) putting in place a Total Quality programme. Fewer people need convincing, fewer people deliberately get in the way to obstruct or defend their corner, and people are on the whole more helpful to those others in their organisation tasked with making the programme happen. So if any of the symptoms in the previous sentence ring a bell, prepare for a pleasant surprise.

155

A business's previous experience will therefore stand it in good stead as far as this book goes. For, no doubt, varying approaches to planning and implementation will have been explored – and varying degrees of success experienced. We cannot here do much beyond merely touch upon all the various management methodologies to do with project planning, employee participation and the whole subject of 'making change happen'. They are hardly, in any case, exact sciences. Whole books have been written on what we have only part of a single chapter for – and most managers and businesses, in any case, have their own ideas on what suits their particular styles and organisations.

What we can do, though, is explore some of the implications

that an environmentally-oriented approach has on these aspects of the change process. Let's start with the decision of what to tackle – and the order to approach it in.

PLAN OF CAMPAIGN

Even before getting on to the question of resources, and who is to do what, it must be obvious that – in all but the smallest or already very green businesses – it's impossible to do everything all at once. So decisions need to be taken. Where does the business start to clean up its act: what comes first – and then second, and third, and so on.

This is a complex decision – far more so than when (say) looking at Total Quality. There are really several things to be considered.

156

- What legal requirements need observing? These must have a high priority – directors can be personally liable for prosecution, employees may be at risk, and practices that are actually outlawed are highly likely to be most injurious to the environment.

- What opportunities are there for immediate- or short-term cost cutting? These will also be high on any business's agenda. The check lists that we have worked through have highlighted commonly applicable opportunities – individual businesses may well find others.

- Which changes make the biggest difference to the environment? Not always an easy one, because sometimes the impact of a change is two-edged. But which offers the best *net* effect?

- What scope is there for making short-term changes that help the way the business is perceived – by customers, employers

and neighbours? Marketing and public relations consequences are important.

- Which short-term changes best suit the resource level at the
  moment? In environmentalism, as in most things, there is a
  'learning curve' effect: what takes a disproportionate
  amount of time today seems easy tomorrow, as skills are
  gained and understanding built on.

- Are the proposed changes ones that bring in the whole range
  of employees? Try to involve as broad a cross section of people
  as possible – it maximises the impact and avoids having
  people feeling left out.

- Is the business a leader – or a laggard? Within your industry
  – yet again, talk to your trade or industry association – most
  businesses will face similar problems. Is yours spearheading
  the way – or does it have a lot of catching up to do?

From all these deliberations will probably emerge a three-tier
list:

- Things to do straightaway – changes that offer immediate
  gains to profits, the environment, public relations and levels
  of legal compliance. Don't feel uncomfortable about the
  public relations element – there's nothing at all wrong with
  letting people and businesses know that you're going
  green . . . provided, of course, that the claims are genuine.

- More medium-term changes – worth doing both in terms of
  the environment, the business's commercial imperatives and
  its external relations, but which take second place to those
  immediate actions that are being tackled straightaway.

- Longer-term improvements to the business's impact on the
  environment. Actions can find themselves put off, not
  because of any particular tardiness or lack of commitment by

a company, but for a variety of quite genuine reasons. Lack of resource. . . large scale capital investment requirements. . . and even diminishing marginal returns. Something may well be worth doing – but dozens of other things ahead of them on the list have an immediate impact. This longer-term list *isn't* a 'put off and never do' list – it's a list of things for your company to fit into its cycles of plant replacement and capital investment.

The important thing is to draw up the list! Agonising over which action comes before what is pointless. And, in contrast to other initiatives that a business may have adopted, such debates are possible. Many initiatives have their own internal logical structure – if a business is adopting Just-in-Time or Total Quality, then certain actions, by the nature of things, need doing before others. If you're building a house, the foundations come before the roof. Not so, necessarily, with an environmental programme, which is more of a broad series of parallel and complementary actions rather than a cross-linked and interdependent structure. With an overall plan of campaign in place, it's time to start getting into the detail of who does what.

ASSIGNING ROLES

This is where the experience gained from previous initiatives really counts. 'We know who we're *not* going to ask to get involved!' But *someone* has to get things moving – the question is, who?

In practice, this depends on the organisation. Environmentalists are sometimes heard proposing that businesses appoint full-time employees to the role of 'environmental officer', charged with ensuring that the greenest possible standards are adhered to. In larger businesses, calls for Environmental Directors are sometimes heard, in order to get proper recognition and resource deployment at the most senior level. Worthy stuff, and appropriate for some businesses, but equally likely to fall on deaf ears in many others, who lack the time, resources, manpower or even inclination.

Thankfully, there's an alternative. Just as having a Quality Director doesn't ensure perfect products, neither will having an Environmental Officer or Director do the trick with the environment. The key to Total Quality – and the thing that makes it work – is that it pushes responsibility down the line to *people*. Quality, instead of becoming someone else's problem, becomes theirs. So get *individuals* involved. Motivate people, explain things to them – and let them loose. This also helps to broaden the spread of roles within the organisation, getting everyone to feel that they're playing a part. Establishing an environmentally aware culture in an organisation is easier if it is constantly self-reinforcing, with everyone knowing that everyone else is doing the same things as they are – switching lights off, re-using or recycling paper and minimising not-strictly-necessary travel.

159

So assign individual roles and responsibilities. Some of these are relatively straightforward: there's usually only one person in an organisation (or at least at any single site in an organisation) who's responsible for catering. There will still however be instances where actions need to be shared or parallel – most parts of the organisation use paper, transport decisions aren't just made by the Transport or Logistics Manager, and so on.

Some responsibilities are genuinely split, though, with no one person having the overall power or authority to make anything happen. The distinction between decisions being split and being shared is crucial. We've just talked about shared decisions: any manager in an organisation may make decisions about (say) the use of recycled paper – although it may need many managers to be involved before it can be said that the organisation as a whole is using it. These are shared, parallel decisions.

But decisions involving (say) anti-pollution measures or the more complex areas of energy efficiency are not so simple. Here, individuals efforts are best pooled. This is a valuable way of working – behavioural scientists know that teams are far more effective at making changes successfully. Academic research with problem solving exercises, for example, shows that almost two-thirds of teams will perform better than the best individual team member on their own – and that virtually *all* teams will perform better than average team members on their own. Which, in the areas of environmental action that we're talking about here, is a pretty powerful argument for bringing people together into teams. Not only are the required actions themselves likely to be complex and cross-functional, but they may also require a team approach to solve. As with so many things, it's not that the problems are necessarily insoluble, but the last thing a business wants is the sledgehammer approach – a problem removed from sight by being sunk under a weight of money and machinery. Solutions of elegant simplicity are sometimes possible – but experience suggests that teams are better at evolving them.

This is not to say that there is *no* role for the Environmental Officer, or even Director. If a business feels its problems and scale merit such, and it can afford it, then fine. But they aren't always necessary – at least on a full-time basis. It may, however, prove useful to have some co-ordinating person to pull the various threads together – and to take responsibility for keeping the Board aware of environmentally related matters. If no obvious candidate seems to be available, a business may feel that a committee would be the best way of having this role performed – the Chair of the committee, in this case, having the responsibility for reporting to the Board on environmental progress and compliance.

Committees – teams, steering groups, call them what you will – also avoid the danger of having the environmental initiative associated with one person. It may then run the risk of getting caught up in office politics, or stalling should the individual leave the business. Committee members should ideally comprise people blessed with a combination of enthusiasm and relevant knowledge. (Obviously, an appropriate level of authority within the business is also important.) In practice, such people are rarely found. So should one go for enthusiastic ignoramuses, or people with the appropriate technical knowledge and acumen, but without the drive to do anything with it?

It's a difficult one. Too much enthusiasm, as well as too little, can be dangerous. A middle course is perhaps best – go for knowledge first, but combined with at least some sympathy towards the objectives. Subsequent 'conversions on the road to Damascus' are not uncommon – leaving the committee actually filled with something close to the ideal mix, but having taken a little time to build up the appropriate head of steam.

161

The choice of people needs also to reflect the different functions within the business. To some extent, the debate is essentially a re-run of the one in Chapter 3 in relation to the audit team. It also depends on the *type* of business involved. An essentially administrative organisation won't have any manufacturing or engineering people, for example.

Try to include people from the following functions:

- purchasing
- the core business function – manufacturing managers, engineering managers, office managers or whatever, according to the nature of your business

- marketing

- finance

- the part of the organisation that is responsible for the business's equipment, buildings and land.

Environmental reporting

Once things are underway, the role of regular environmental reporting is to help the business monitor how it is progressing towards meeting its green policy objectives. Some businesses and organisations – at the larger end of the spectrum, admittedly – go into tremendous detail, producing glossy brochures for dissemination to employees, the public and external parties with which it trades or does business. For the typical organisation, though, such lengths are probably unnecessary – although quite possibly very useful in the case of businesses operating in environmentally sensitive areas, or close to neighbours that it wishes to stay on good terms with.

A regular environmental statement – say on an annual basis – does help everyone make sure that they've still got their eyes on the ball. List the policy objectives, detail the actions that have been taken towards meeting them in the year, and – most importantly – list those actions to be taken in the following year. The following environmental statement then records compliance against these.

As businesses increasingly communicate more and more with their employees and the outside world – plenty of businesses now produce company newsletters, magazines and the like – this sort of reporting finds a ready and interested audience. Publish extracts on company noticeboards as well – along with interim progress reports throughout the year.

Try to incorporate the business's environmental objectives into the regular management reporting systems. Progress towards quality, health and safety and personnel objectives are probably reported already: add the environmental ones to the list.

Setting the standard

1992 saw the introduction of BS7750 in the UK. It's a general – and voluntary – environmental management standard for companies to adopt and work to. The name of standard – BS7750 – is quite deliberately intended to reinforce the link to quality systems standard BS5750. Indeed, part of the standard quite explicitly lists the actual links between the two. And just as all sorts of businesses and organisations are adopting BS5750 – voluntarily, or because their trading partners have asked them to – an equally wide range of firms will find BS7750 appropriate. Banks, publishers, software houses, factories, distributors – there's something in it for all of them.

163

The purpose of the standard is in some ways similar to the UK's Environmental Protection Act. It doesn't list in detail what and what not to do, but specifies the elements of a recommended *environmental management system*. In drafting it, its authors intended the standard to be one that organisations already working to BS5750 could readily extend their systems to cope with – although they are at pains to stress that BS5750 is not a prerequisite for BS7750. Just as with BS5750, independent outside organisations can assist a firm in adopting the standard, and in granting an audited statement of compliance with it.

The standard is still fairly new, and many businesses are just becoming aware of it. Nevertheless, its significance will only increase.

Spreading the message

Having done all this you'll want to consolidate the gains to the business and to the environment in your organisation. You're up to speed, and now need to keep abreast of new developments and feed ideas into the regular planning process of your business. Remember, you've done all the work to understand how your buisness affects the environment – you've set out a plan and clear priorities. New developments and ideas just have to be fed into this existing framework. Your organisation now has a system that enables decisions on continuing to build an environmentally sound business to be made on a clear business basis. Will this new idea bring environmental benefits? Test ideas against your plans – if they fit then go ahead – and help your business and the environment.

Of course, the environment is everyone's. You'll want to encourage others to play their part too. Perhaps your business is already a member of a local business organisation – if so, why not encourage it to spread the word to other members. If not, how about joining (or even setting up some meetings), and keeping environmental management on the agenda. Remember, you have a story to tell – not just of success, but of problems and how your business overcame them. And if everything's plain sailing in the future, you'll probably be unique. Sharing problems with colleagues in other businesses often helps you to overcome them. And by getting the organisations with which you do business – suppliers, contractors, and so on – to take the same approach, you'll also reduce the overall environmental impacts of your business. In the interdependent environment we live in, it's not just what happens inside your factory fence that matters, it's the whole sequence from obtaining raw materials to the final disposal of used products – from the cradle-to-grave – that matters. Control your firm's environmental effects, and encourage others to do the same, and the environment benefits even more.

Work through your network of business contacts to spread the message. Remember too, your other networks – for example your contacts with stakeholders mentioned earlier in this chapter. Your firm's commitment to environmentally sound business management will influence them, too!

First of all, your employees will be noticing a difference: energy efficient lightbulbs, perhaps; or paper and waste recycling; or use of environmentally-sound primary materials. Some of their suggestions may even help your firm achieve the priorities that it has set itself. But just as importantly, your example is likely to encourage them to try the same ideas in their homes and outside work. Perhaps there are ways you can help this process along – maybe by encouraging car-sharing to come to work, or use of public transport. One firm I know in London has even gone so far as to buy its staff bikes, written off over five years. Perhaps staff want to put in the same type of energy-efficient lighting you're using at work, in their homes, but can't find a place to buy them. How about ordering a few more than your firm needs and selling them to employees who want them?

165

And any business, large or small, can help environmental organisations directly with funding by creating a 'give as you earn' scheme for its employees, who can then regularly make a monthly donation from their salaries. Again, a business may choose to top this up with a further sum – perhaps on a per-centage basis.

You will also be influencing your customers, perhaps offering a new environmentally-sounder alternative to their current pur-chases, and your local council. Talking to them won't just help spread the word, but may well increase their commitment to your enterprise. So let people know your commitment to environmental management. In short, good environmental management is good business practice – and people want to deal with good businesses.

Appendix 1

■

Gas Condensing Boilers:

Caradon Heating Ltd
PO Box 103
National Avenue
Hull
HU5 4JN
Tel: 0482 492251

Gas Consumers Council:

Alford House
15 Wilton Road
London
SW1V 1LT
Tel: 071 931 0977

General information:

Department of Energy's Energy Efficiency Office
Department of Trade and Industry
1 Palace Street
London
SW1E 5HE
Tel: 071 215 5000

The Energy Efficiency Office guide *Practical Energy Saving Guide for Smaller Businesses*, 1992, is an excellent starting point for your company's energy management.

Information on air conditioning and refrigeration plant without CFCs

Elstree Air Conditioning
12 Vincent Avenue
Crownhill Business Centre
Crownhill
Milton Keynes
MK8 0AB
Tel: 0908 261933

British Gas
326 High Holborn
London
WC1V 7PT
Tel: 071 821 1444

Carrier Corporation (United Technologies)
Syracuse
New York
USA
Tel: 0101-203-674-3132

Information on improving vehicle efficiency:

'Fuel Saving'
Department of Transport
Publicity Stores
Building No 3
Victoria Road
South Ruislip
Middlesex
HA4 0NZ

Information on Wind Energy:

British Wind Energy Association
4 Hamilton Place
London
W1V 0BQ

OFGAS (Office of Gas Supply):

Southside
105 Victoria Street
London
SW1E 6QT
Tel: 071 828 0898

Oil Condensing Boiler Manufacturer:

Yorkpark Ltd
16 St George's Industrial Estate
White Lion Road
Amersham
Bucks
HP7 9JQ
Tel: 0494 764031

169

Index

■